Spilled Gravy

Spilled Gravy

Advice on
Love, Life, and Acceptance

from a Man
Uniquely Unqualified
to Give It

ED DRISCOLL

◼ HAZELDEN®

Hazelden, Center City, Minnesota 55012-0176
1-800-328-0094
1-651-213-4590 (Fax)
www.hazelden.org

Library of Congress Cataloging-in-Publication Data

Driscoll, Ed, 1961-
   Spilled gravy: advice on love, life, and acceptance from a man uniquely
   unqualified to give it / Ed Driscoll.
      p. cm.
   ISBN-13: 978-1-59285-353-3 (softcover)
   ISBN-10: 1-59285-353-6 (softcover)
   1. Driscoll, Ed, 1961- 2. Television comedy writers--United States--
Biography. I. Title.

   PN1992.4.D75A3 2006
   812'.6--dc22
   [B]
                                                                    2005055041

This book shares the personal experiences of the author. In some cases,
he has changed names and circumstances to protect the privacy of his
friends and family.

10 09 08 07 06   6 5 4 3 2 1

Cover design by Theresa Gedig
Interior design by Ann Sudmeier
Typesetting by Stanton Publication Services, Inc.

Dedicated to the
loving memory of
Peggy and Ed Driscoll Sr.

Contents

Foreword

Spilled Gravy. Now doesn't that sound like something I might be involved with? I usually don't write forewords to books, not because I think I am above it, but because I am so lazy. I've known Driscoll (that's what I call him) for quite a while. He told me he was writing a book, so I said, "Hey, I'd love to read it." You know, just being polite. And the next thing you know, here I am, me and my big mouth, writing the foreword. But, boy, I'm glad I am. Driscoll has written a book that looks at life in the same way I tend to look at it. Not just stories that make you laugh, but stories that take you on a ride — from the ups and downs of life, to the challenges of recovery, to the ins and outs of big-time show business. He writes with honesty, candor, and humor about his sometimes painful inner search for meaning. Driscoll takes a straight look into his life mirror, and he shows the willingness to make changes that aren't easy but are necessary if he is to revisit that mirror.

After reading Driscoll's soon-to-be best seller, I must say I now know him better and deeper. He is a great comedian, a great comedy writer, and now a wonderful author. I am glad to know him and honored to write this foreword. I will stop writing now because no foreword should be longer than one page, especially if I have to write it. Let me just say, you'll never look at gravy the same way.

Louie Anderson

Acknowledgments

I would like to thank the many people who enabled me to write this book, some with their technical expertise, and others who helped simply by giving me their unconditional support. I'd like to name them all, but the list would probably be longer than the book itself, which I've been told is not a great selling point. However, I definitely need to thank the following: Edward Driscoll Sr. and Margaret Driscoll, for being attracted to each other enough to give birth to me, and for the rock-solid values they taught me and my sisters. And oh, yeah, I guess I'd better mention my sisters, too, or they'll probably stiff me on my Christmas gifts: Kathleen Driscoll, Colleen Braim, and Maureen Watko. Thanks also to Tom Braim, Neil Watko, my nephews Sean Watko and Ross Watko, my dear friends Maggie Adams, Jeanne Basse, Dina Conway, Nick Rosenbach, as well as Varol and Kim Ablak, Bill and Nancy Braudis, and Jim and Lori Moore and their wonderful families. Thanks to Louie Anderson, Billy Crystal, David Steinberg, and Dennis Miller, for their help and guidance in my career. A special thanks to Helga Schier, without whose editing prowess this book would be one long run-on sentence. Also, a huge thanks to my manager and close friend Ahmos Hassan and his wonderful wife, Tina, and son, Ramses.

I could never have written *Spilled Gravy* without the love and support of all these incredible people. So if you don't like the book, please blame them.

Chapter
⁂ 1 ⁂

Putting the "Ed" in Education

I really don't know what happened. I'll probably spend a good portion of the rest of my days wondering how she went from "I can't wait to carry your child," to "Everything you do sucks." Since we've broken up for good, I don't expect Rita will be dropping by anytime soon, except perhaps to reclaim the cutlery she's stored in my back.

But that's good, because now I'm starting a new life! Instead of getting bogged down in the soul-numbing sadness of the situation, I've determined that I will make the best use of my new freedom. I'll take time between stand-up performances and television writing to do the things necessary to vastly improve my life.

Starting today, I'll work out every morning, read classic literature for one hour each afternoon, organize all my records, go to my Twelve Step meetings, donate time to the local soup kitchen, work on my screenplay, and just generally become the Renaissance man I've always known I was deep inside.

Twenty-four hours later of PlayStation and jerking off, I realized that I was once again experiencing the state of confusion that always comes over me when a relationship inevitably goes awry. You'd think I'd know how to handle it by now. It's been the same story for most of my thirty-nine years.

⋚ ⋚

I was never particularly adept at handling women, even in the suave, debonair days of first grade. I developed my initial heavy-duty trust issue when I caught my first girlfriend eating paste with another boy during nap-time. And like many teenagers, I had my first serious sexual relationship with a stack of *National Geographics* in the family basement.

My parents were, and continue to be, wonderful people. Growing up in Pittsburgh, we were basically the Cleaver family, though Mom rarely wore a dress and pearls when cleaning the house. My parents are extremely honest, undoubtedly too honest for me at times. Once, when I was about fifteen, I had a bout of dysentery on a night that I had planned to go out with some buddies. Imagine my horror when, as I sat on the throne, I heard my mother answer the door down the hall and say to my friends, "Sorry, Eddie can't come out tonight; he has diarrhea." My chin sunk to my chest, because I knew what was in store for me. I complained to my mother, but she dismissed my concerns, saying "It's a natural body function, nothing to be ashamed of."

God love Mom, she naively expected a group of teenagers to have the same level of maturity as her bridge club. Sure enough, for the next six months or so, whenever there was a lull in a conversation among my friends, or somebody was guarding me in basketball, or I was trying to talk to some pretty girl, or any other moment that begged for commentary, someone would inevitably pipe up with, "Eddie has diarrhea."

I have three older sisters, and even the family beagle was female. Sadly, being surrounded by females didn't help me understand the gender any better than if I'd been raised in a monastery.

When as a child I started asking questions about girls, my rather conservative parents weren't particularly eager to discuss such things. One day my father sat me down and with an ominously serious look, said, "So, your mother says you want to know about the birds and the bees." Confused, I replied, "No, I want to know about sex. Like, what are blow jobs?"

Once the color came back to his face, Dad sputtered, "You'll have sex ed this year . . . I don't mean you'll have *sex*, Ed, this year . . . I'm saying you'll have *sex education* this year . . . so, you'll find out at school." With that, he turned and practically leaped out of the room.

And I did find out at school, but not from the teachers. It was from fellow fifth-grader Paul Murawski, who explained to me earnestly, "There's a seed inside a girl, and the guy puts his dinky in there and pees on it." I always thought Paul had a future as a romantic song lyricist.

It seemed unlikely I'd find out much about sex in the classrooms at Our Lady of Grace grade school. The only thing they taught us about sex was that it's dirty. And I suppose that's all we really needed to know at that point. In a way, it was a relief to know one would likely never get past "first base" in elementary school. It was hard enough just to talk to girls without introducing sex into the already overwhelming equation.

Incredibly, being the fifth-grade chess champion didn't win me much favor with the babes but did entitle me to several ass-kickings at recess by the school bullies, free of charge.

I did my best to get girls' attention. Though I wore braces and glasses and was smaller than most of the boys and half of the girls, I joined the football team. I figured it was the best way to meet the cheerleaders.

Our team was coached by Mr. Jackson, a zealous individual who saw his leadership of a group of seventh- and eighth-grade boys as a natural springboard to coaching in the NFL. It used to make me laugh when he'd shout, "Nobody scores on the Our Lady of Grace defense!" Not exactly intimidating. It would have made sense if we were Our Lady of Chastity, i.e., "Nobody scores on Our Lady of Chastity."

It was also unnerving to heckle other teams in the Catholic league. Yelling "Holy Ghost sucks!" seemed a certain ticket to hell. I wanted to win, sure, but not at the cost of my soul.

Coach Jackson had a myriad of bizarre motivational tools that he employed. For instance, the week of the big rivalry with crosstown St. Bernard's, he put decals with the letters "P-R-I-D" on our helmets and told us that we'd get the letter "E" after we proved we had "pride" by winning the game. Sadly, we went into the locker room at halftime down 42–0, and I rearranged the letters on my helmet to read "D-R-I-P." This so enraged Mr. Jackson that he busted his clipboard over my head. The noise that reverberated inside my helmet was similar to someone jamming live grenades into my ear holes.

Word of Coach Jackson's outburst toward me spread quickly. It was the biggest buzz in the school since Leonard Fabrizi stole his dad's bag of "Mail Pouch" tobacco and brought it to school, whereupon Paul Bammenstreider swallowed a huge chunk and vomited in the auditorium.

I don't mean to dwell on such scatological events, but vomiting certainly was a major part of grade school. It seemed like every other day somebody would do "the liquid laugh." I'm glad kids seem to grow out of that. It sure would be a drag if constant barfing continued into adulthood. I can just picture CEOs losing it on the conference table during important board meetings.

The most spectacular "Technicolor yawn" incident I'll always remember occurred at the very end of a school day in second grade. We'd always close the afternoon by singing a religious song, and one afternoon we rose and began singing "Immaculate Mary, your praises we— *SPLAT!*"

Mark Thomas had vomited on Patty Peternell's hand, and she screamed and raced around the room, holding her limp arm away from her body in complete horror, as though it had been dipped in nuclear waste. To this day, when I hear the song "Immaculate Mary" in church, I can practically smell the Lysol.

As far as the coach hitting me over the head, I wasn't really fazed. I was thwacked fairly often in elementary school. Once, in sixth grade, the principal, Sister Ardath, whom we referred to as "Sister Adolph," decided that we were too noisy at lunchtime, so she canceled recess and made us stand at attention in the cafeteria. That was understandable, don't you think? After all, when you have a group of overly energetic children, the best thing to do is keep them confined in as small a space as possible. You don't want them going outside; they'd only blow off steam out there.

When Sister Ardath left the cafeteria and ordered us to remain standing against the wall, I convinced the rest of the class that we should put our hands up on our heads like prisoners of war. One by one we did so, and when Sister Adolph returned, she was greeted by the site of a line of eleven-year-olds looking as if they were about to face a firing squad. She immediately charged up to me, grabbed me around the throat, and hissed,

"You, Mr. Driscoll, are 50 percent of the sixth grade's problem." To which I replied, "I'd like to think it's more like seventy-five."

All the kids laughed, and she hauled off and slapped me across the face, which I considered worth the big laugh I'd gotten. It actually got me a pity kiss from Kelly Grant, but when I gingerly tried for a second kiss, Kelly hit me harder than Adolph had.

Looking back with the 20/20 clarity that only hindsight can provide, I probably should have seen that getting slapped by Kelly was a huge signpost, warning me of the heartaches that the pursuit of love inevitably brings with it. If I'd only understood that her reaction was indicative of just how unpredictable relationships with the opposite sex tend to be, I might have saved myself a lot of trouble, not to mention my face.

≷ ≶

Here I sit in my new house. Well, new to me, anyway. It was built in 1927, and the couple who lived here previously had occupied the house since, oh, roughly 1927. Okay, maybe not that long, but long enough so that I have to replace the carpets, drapes, and anything else that could possibly collect that "old people smell" with new stuff that would soon collect my own "middle-aged person smell." Yep, new window dressing, new colors, new furniture, but . . . the porta-potty set up in a corner of the kitchen stays. I like efficient use of time.

Being in Los Angeles, I was advised by my Realtor to

make everything in my house "earthquake-ready," which I guess means make sure everything is ready to be shattered in the event of an earthquake. I mean, really, there's only so much humankind can do in the face of nature's fury. It's obviously out of our control. I did, however, store my saber collection directly above my bed, just as a precaution.

This is a pretty big place, certainly for one person living alone, which is my new role in life. Rita called off our wedding, luckily only after I'd spent tens of thousands of dollars on a diamond ring. Imagine how bad I'd feel if five prime years of my life WEREN'T completely wasted. But, I've let it go. . . . Except, I have to ask, why was I the last one to know that Rita and I even had any problems? It was just a few months before we were to be married when she called me into the living room so that we could "talk." Right there, I should have been suspicious. The phrases *We have to talk* or *Let's talk* are always indicative that a tense, uncomfortable conversation is about to take place. After all, when there's no problem, nobody talks about talking. They just talk.

Rita informed me that she wanted to "postpone" the wedding. I was completely stunned, which tells you how well communication between us had worked so far. She told me she was unhappy, and I made the huge mistake of asking, "Why?" She immediately launched into a litany of things that I did wrong, including not putting the spoons back in the proper drawer in the kitchen. Well, this was great. O. J. Simpson had women lining up to date him, but because I wasn't filing the silverware properly, suddenly I'm Ike Turner? I stood there and took it like a man as she went down her list of grievances.

"Another thing," she said, her voice quivering, "I don't understand your obsession with watching football." She said this with the thorough disgust someone might say, "I don't understand your obsession with child pornography." Somehow, despite being with me for four years, she hadn't realized that I was a big sports fan until just recently. I guess I shouldn't have been hiding it by watching all those games in front of her.

Rita was sobbing and complaining for a solid half hour or so, and my head was spinning. Here I thought I had finally gotten past my instinctive disdain and fear of relationships, thinking I had found "the one," only to have "the one" dump this whole thing in my lap.

We went to couples counseling, which, I've come to realize in retrospect, is merely an expensive way to find out that your relationship sucks. Counseling did help somewhat, however. It's where I learned it's better to say, "Could you put your dirty dishes away?" instead of "I've been combing through the bylaws of LA county, and you'll be surprised to know that there's no statute saying you can't put your dishes in the dishwasher."

Counseling went badly from our very first session, during which Rita blurted out, "How do I know that when we have kids and I need help with them, you won't be too busy watching football?" My mature response was, "Well, how do I know that you won't suddenly start wearing face-paint and insist on being called 'Zoltar'? I guess we just don't know, do we?" The counselor immediately informed me that I wasn't being helpful. (Who knew? I guess that's why she's a doctor.) But even Rita had to admit that this fear seemed unfounded, because though I am a rabid sports fan, it had never interfered with anything she had asked me to do. Frankly, I was quite insulted by her insinuation, as if one day she'd be in the kitchen screaming, "Our child just climbed in the oven!" and I'd be in the den shouting, "Hang on, it's fourth and two."

If she was going to concoct some future, horrible behavior she was afraid I'd engage in, it could have at least been something grounded in reality. Like maybe me taking off on a three-day Scotch bender. Which, as we sat through one uncomfortable counseling session after another, began more and more to sound like a pretty good plan. It soon became clear that no amount of professional doctoring could bring the dead patient that was Rita and Ed's relationship back to life.

⤝ ⤜

When I was in grade school, my best friend John Maurer and I were both far more interested in making people laugh than impressing the girls. We spent virtually every minute of our free time pulling ridiculous hijinks. To the girls, our juvenile exploits merely made us appear, well, juvenile. But as far as I was concerned, if the girls didn't "get it," it was their loss.

A typically mature slice of fun we used to serve up every weekend was to go into Woolworth's, grab onto a spool of yarn, and start dragging it with us around the store, zigzagging down various aisles, forming a giant yarn web to entrap the other shoppers.

We also spent a lot of time listening to comedy records, and by the time I was fourteen, I had memorized all of Robert Klein's albums, particularly *Child of the 50's,* which I still consider the funniest album ever made. Klein came to Pittsburgh to open for Helen Reddy at a large theater called the Syria Mosque, and my sister and I went to the show. Klein was as great as I expected, but sadly, most of the crowd was there to hear Helen roar—in numbers too big to ignore. Though the audience was receptive to Klein, I got a lot of puzzled looks from people as I stood and clapped and laughed and hollered during his performance.

Little could I have known that ten years later, I myself would be the opening act for Robert Klein when he played Pittsburgh. I felt so awkward when I met him, trying to act cool, as if I were a peer, and in the next breath asking him to autograph all my albums. He was incredibly gracious to me, and today those signed records hang proudly on the wall of my living room.

But back in 1975, inspired by Klein's work, long before I had actually met him, I entered the eighth-grade talent show. I knocked 'em dead with an impression of our gym teacher, Mr. Schwartz, perfectly mimicking his staccato speech patterns and quirky physical movements. It was then that I realized I might actually have a future with what eventually would become my true love: comedy.

≥ ≤

It rained the entire day I moved into this house because, well, I was moving, and rain was the most hellish condition Mother Nature could work up for me on such short notice. It was almost oddly comforting, because it was so consistent with the unpleasant nature of my life since the breakup with Rita. As I attempted to settle in, the house was freezing, because *surprise!* the central heating system had broken down. With amazing prescience (a fancy word for saying I knew crappy stuff would inevitably happen), I had signed up for a house appliance insurance policy, and for a yearly fee, anytime I had a problem I could call a central toll-free number, and a repair person would be dispatched for the maximum price of $35.

So, in the morning, rubbing the sleep out of my blue eyes and even bluer skin, I dialed up the central number and, teeth chattering like a Buddy Rich solo, explained that my house was very cold because my heater wasn't working.

The woman on the phone asked, "What's wrong with it?"

I explained, "You know how the heater's supposed to give out heat? It's not." This answer seemed to satisfy her, but then things *really* got icy. It turns out the central office is located in Minnesota, and when she typed in my policy number it revealed that I live in LA.

"Uh, you're in California, right?"

"Yes."

"And you're telling me it's cold? What, is it down to seventy or something?" A pretty funny line, actually, and

I would have laughed out loud had my voice box not been frozen. "Listen," I pleaded. "It's forty degrees in my house, and that's cold no matter where you live. Forty degrees is forty degrees, even in LA. It's not like the time difference. No conversion necessary."

She wasn't convinced. "You're telling me it can get that cold out there?"

You'd think I was calling from some distant, exotic planet. I completely snapped. "Oh, yes, we've got cold, and rain, and sunshine, and air, too! But the sky is made of chocolate! Fish walk among us, and the trees speak out loud! I'm calling from inside a toadstool at this very moment. It's a land of intrigue and magic!" As she hung up loudly in my ear, I thought, *Gee, I feel warmer already.*

Fortunately, when I called back, I got a different woman. I'm pretty sure I did, but I disguised my voice anyway, just in case. I was told a repairman would be at my house the following day between 7 a.m. and noon. Just like clockwork, that next day, the repairman pounded on my door at 6 a.m. sharp. Just as I was stepping into the shower.

≥ ≤

For the most part, I enjoyed high school immensely. I really didn't think I would at first, because most of the kids from Our Lady of Grace went off to a school called Chartiers Valley, while I was one of only six students who went to Upper St. Clair High. Attending my first public school and hardly knowing a soul was a daunting proposition. Fortunately, I was able to use my sense of humor for a myriad of purposes, everything from joking my way past bullies, to meeting new friends, to chatting with girls. It was in ninth grade that I began to realize just how useful being funny could be in everyday life. Largely through humor, I became pretty popular at Upper St. Clair High and made friends with people I'm still close to today.

Like most young men, I desperately wanted to be a jock, but despite my best efforts, I wasn't much of an athlete. The fact that I was such a sports fan but lacked any actual playing ability had always been a glancing blow to my adolescent psyche, but by twelfth grade I'd accepted it and realized I should concentrate on the gifts I did have, most notably my sense of humor.

I ran track my senior year, and I was a triple threat with my slowness of foot, limited lung power, and general lack of coordination. I basically became the team mascot, and I enjoyed hanging around and keeping the team loose. Mr. Cline, the head track coach, seemed to find me amusing and encouraged my joking around.

The highlight of track season was when we all traveled to a big meet in Slippery Rock, Pennsylvania. One of my teammates, Mark Smith, had left some equipment in one of the buses, and when he went back to retrieve it, he discovered the female bus driver performing oral sex on the male bus driver. The startled couple pleaded for Mark to have mercy and show discretion, which Mark did. He waited nearly ten whole seconds before telling the entire team.

Perhaps because we were so distracted, we finished

dead last among a group of schools we were expected to beat easily. On the drive back home, we all displayed our maturity by pretending to cough as we yelled "blow job." Our poor coaches tried to keep us in order as desperately as they tried to suppress their own laughter.

At the awards banquet at the end of the year, Mr. Cline asked me to make some remarks. I was more than happy to do so. I stood up at the podium and said, "I think we all remember Slippery Rock, when we weren't the only ones who 'blew the meet.'" The parents were baffled by the team's explosive reaction. I then made the unfortunate choice of following up with, "They should call it 'Slippery Cock.'" I hadn't yet learned to edit myself for my audience.

High school was when I really began performing in earnest, though it was not in any of the plays or usual productions of *Oklahoma!* that most aspiring show business people get involved in. While I secretly admired the kids who did act in the plays, I preferred to hang back and good-naturedly make fun of them. Eventually, I was approached by Mr. Harshman, an affable fellow who oversaw the theater department. He said, "I hear you're a funny guy. Why don't you ever try out for any of the plays?" I told him I didn't want to seem snobbish, but that I preferred to do my own material. "Not to be cocky, but I think I'm much funnier than Rodgers and Hammerstein."

He found this amusing and told me that he was starting a program called "Traveling Troupe," which would consist of a group of students who would perform at various community functions. They would play at the chamber of commerce dinner, Rotary Club, Elks, PTA gatherings, in other words, at any event where people were unwilling to pay for REAL entertainment. Mr. Harshman informed me that they had singers, dancers, guitarists, kids doing dramatic monologues, but no comedians. Right away, then, he'd appealed to something I'm always interested in: lack of competition. I agreed to work up a routine and join the troupe.

This presented a problem. You see, I didn't really have a "routine." Yeah, I was the school clown, but I realized that holding forth in the cafeteria about how sloppy Ricky is when he eats might not translate to a group of Rotarians. I'd have to come up with a real routine. Some of my friends suggested doing some of the bits from one of Klein's or George Carlin's records. But even at that age, I knew that to present other's humor as my own was wrong. (Unfortunately, some of my peers today, both comedians and writers, feel no such qualms about doing this.) No, though it was tempting to perform proven stuff from the masters, I felt that I needed to make my own way.

My first audience may have regretted that sense of ethics. The Elks club folks were polite, but the response was rightly muted. I think they enjoyed my sheer audacity more than my jokes. Because I was worried sick about having to memorize anything, I decided to use the old comedy staple of reading a fake newscast, à la "Weekend Update." My opening line consisted of me saying, "And now it's time for some news briefs," and producing a giant pair of my father's underwear. (Actually, I could probably sell this bit to Carrot Top today.) Though the laughs weren't huge, the crowd gave me a big hand when I was finished, though, in retrospect, they may have just been relieved that I was done.

All things considered, I enjoyed the experience. To actually have been introduced as a "comedian" to a group of people I didn't know, and to have more or less entertained them made me feel like a "real" comedian. Mr. Harshman was very encouraging, and when I reported to my parents that all had gone fairly well at the Elks club, they were pleased. Dad even seemed proud that I was using HIS underwear in my act.

Eventually, I learned how to tweak jokes, how to deliver them, how to anticipate what would probably get a laugh and what probably wouldn't. By the time I graduated, I had become pretty comfortable onstage.

As for offstage, well, I had the usual interest in girls that sixteen-year-olds do, but found the whole dating thing confusing, anxiety-inducing, and downright painful. Little did I know that it would only become worse as I got older.

Sure, I dated, but things never seemed to click. For whatever reason, I'm one of those guys who always got along with my girlfriend's parents better than I got along with my girlfriend. I remember one girl, Kara, whose folks were the best. Whenever I was over there, they'd bring us snacks and let us watch the giant screen TV. I actually liked hanging out with them. I'll admit it got a bit awkward, though, when later, after I'd broken up with Kara, I started showing up at their house with other women I was dating.

I went out with some terrific girls, but even at that age it seemed to me that relationships were always destined to end in one of two brutal ways: either I hurt her, or she hurt me. I remember making the conscious decision in high school to never get too serious with a female. In truth, this was probably because, like most teenagers, I was scared to death of the whole dating process. But it was far easier to tell myself that I was merely being prudent, because a relationship would only get in the way of the comedy career I planned to have.

≶ ≶

It's a good thing my central heating was repaired. That made it a lot easier to take a cold shower the next day when my hot water tank literally exploded. I'm not sure which was worse: the Scud missile–like sound the water tank made as it shattered my back window, or having to once again call the appliance insurance people in Minnesota. Surely I'd be viewed as the malcontent I am, and they'd cancel my policy. Using yet another voice just in case that same woman from before answered, I asked for a plumber as soon as possible.

"First thing Monday morning."

Which would have been great, except that this was Friday afternoon, and I knew I might have the weird urge to clean myself at some point during the weekend. If I wanted to take cold showers, I'd move back in with my ex-fiancée. I was informed that "plumbers don't like to work Saturday mornings," obviously unlike the rest of us who relish the thought. I realized that I really had to let the customer service rep have it. So, I did—I begged and cried like a schoolgirl, and they agreed to send the plumber Saturday morning.

After that call, since I'd gotten what I wanted, a feeling of contentment settled over me. (Or perhaps it was just a mild form of heatstroke from the central air now stuck on the "lava" setting.) But my self-satisfaction was as short-lived as a Colombian president. I received a notice in my mailbox announcing that the city was having a parade Saturday, and it was coming directly down my street. Normally, I would enjoy a gathering of fat Shriners on mopeds and clowns who would have scared John Wayne Gacy, but they were shutting down my street Saturday morning to *all* traffic. Plumbers excluded? I doubted it. *It's March,* I thought. *What could be the occasion for a parade?* The answer to this couldn't be found on the flyer itself. So, once again I talked to my friends in Minnesota and asked if the plumber could be dispatched in the afternoon instead of the morning. The service rep asked me "What's the parade for?"

"Uh, the 'Festival of Inconvenience,'" I sputtered. Surprisingly, they were reluctant to send someone out at a later time because "plumbers don't like to work Saturday afternoons."

I said, "Okay, then. They don't like to work mornings or afternoons. How about at night?"

"Oh, absolutely not, sir."

"So you're saying your plumbers are available anytime except mornings, afternoons, or evenings."

"Yes."

I remained silent for a moment, hoping she might grasp my predicament. But her reciprocal silence told me she either didn't get it or didn't care, so I pressed on.

"So, is there some sort of time warp you'd suggest that we meet in?"

Finally, she took pity on me and agreed to send the plumber out sometime Saturday "after the morning."

The following afternoon, a plumbing van made its way down my street, rolling through the trash left scattered about from the "Have Pride in Your Neighborhood" parade. The driver realized that he had the proper address when he saw the numbers on my mailbox. Unfortunately, he only saw my mailbox after he'd plowed his truck into it while looking for my address. He managed to replace the old water tank with a new one and asked if he could use my bathroom before he left. "Certainly," I said, "I know plumbers love leaks." I laughed. He stared at me blankly.

Several hours after the plumber left, I discovered that he'd tracked mud spots across my new white carpet, making it look as though my floor was covered by a giant Dalmatian pelt. Of course, when I made an accusatory phone call, both he and his supervisor denied any culpability.

As the cumulative effect of all this nonsense began to weigh on me heavily, I became increasingly frustrated. This wasn't how things were supposed to go. More unsettling, however, was the fact that I'd been through far more serious challenges and problems in my life and had come through with my peace of mind intact. Why was I now feeling so miserable, so hopeless? Sure, a lot of little annoyances, mostly with the house, can grate on you, but the angst I was feeling deep inside certainly didn't seem commensurate with these rather pedestrian problems.

≳ ≲

I got my first exposure to critics back in high school. I would occasionally do the morning announcements, which were broadcast over the school intercoms to mostly disinterested students and teachers. I would make flippant remarks about school events and throw in jokes about the head principal's tie. My classmates weren't shy about hunting me down in the hallway later to tell me which jokes they felt weren't up to speed.

I've always hated to be critiqued, always bristled at any kind of feedback that seemed negative to me. Even feedback that is meant as positive I often interpret as disapproving. With this in mind, it's certainly ironic that I eventually chose to go into a line of work that is predicated on nothing but the opinions and feedback of others.

Luckily, my teachers generally enjoyed my humor and let me do a lot of things I probably wouldn't have gotten away with otherwise. I did have a knack for knowing when I could get away with a comment in class and when I couldn't. However, I occasionally misjudged.

One day in class, Mr. D'Alessandro was assigning weekend projects to his students. He said, "Ed, I'm going to ask you to write a report on Fort Pitt." And I said, "And I'm going to ask you to the prom. Let's see which event is more likely to happen." Everyone laughed, including Mr. D. So you can imagine my surprise when he then asked me to step out into the hall with him.

"Am I in trouble or something?" I asked.

"Not yet. Listen, Ed. You're really funny; I have to tell you, I often repeat things you say in my class to the other teachers." Wow, he repeated my jokes to the other teachers? I must really be onto something.

"But the problem is," he continued, "you say something, everyone laughs, then it takes forever to settle everyone down, which makes it tough for me to do my job. I need you to exercise more self-control."

Relieved that I wasn't being suspended, I promised to cooperate. As I went back to my seat, I mimed gluing my lips shut to the rest of the class, which brought more laughter that I hadn't intended. I looked at Mr. D. sheepishly, and he rolled his eyes. Incidentally, I turned in a great report on Fort Pitt the following Monday. But I attended the prom by myself.

It wasn't just my own classes that I felt compelled to entertain. I often dropped by friends' classes, taught by teachers I didn't even know, to do something whimsical. Once a week I stood in the hall outside a friend's English class and did impressions through the vents in the closed door. I started out doing Slim Whitman, since his yodeling records were a popular infomercial at the time, but the novelty of that wore off after a few weeks, and I became desperate to come up with something new. My most spectacular failure was an ill-advised attempt to impersonate Don Ho, complete with bubbles that blew back in my face, causing me to gag and temporarily blinding me.

Fortunately, there were several successful "gigs," such as hosting a "Dating Game" involving a slew of area schools, which was held in our school's auditorium. At several track meets, after I'd come huffing across the finish line, trailing a bunch of other kids, one of them would say, "Hey, didn't you host that Dating Game? You were funny." It almost made up for the humiliation of finishing behind a guy with an artificial leg.

High school is also where I was introduced to an extremely popular peer among the students, known as alcohol. I guess that means I was a late starter, at least by what seem to be today's harrowing standards. When I was sixteen, a couple friends and I had our first twelve-pack of beer. We wandered around the neighborhood on a Friday night, tossing them back and becoming increasingly stupid. The next thing I remember, I woke up in my bedroom. My head was pounding, and I had a vague recollection of stumbling home that night. I somehow was fairly certain that I hadn't tipped off my folks, so I knew my objective for the morning was to go downstairs to the breakfast table and pretend that nothing was out of the ordinary.

There was one small problem: My eyesight is terrible and has been since I was in third grade. Thus, the first thing I did every morning, even before getting out of bed, was to reach over to my nightstand and put my glasses on. Unfortunately, when I reached over that particular morning, my glasses were nowhere to be found. I desperately stumbled around my bedroom, praying to find them, but to no avail. The realization sank in that pretending nothing was out of the ordinary in front of Mom and Dad was going to be even tougher. I now had to do it not only with a foggy head, but with foggy eyes as well. I gathered myself and went downstairs, greeting my folks with a cheery, "Good morning!" My dad looked up from his paper and immediately asked, "Where's your glasses?"

"Oh, they're upstairs," I lied. Right. They were upstairs; it's just that I'd decided to walk around the house blind as a bat that day, just for kicks. It took my dad less than a minute to get the truth out of me. I admitted that I must have lost them at some point when we were wandering drunkenly around the neighborhood.

My mother was horrified, my father disgusted, my sisters amused. "Go get in the car!" Dad barked. I wasn't sure what this meant. I thought he was going to take me out and shoot me or something. At that point, it would have been a relief.

"Why do you want me in the car?" I asked.

"Because we're going to drive around until we find your glasses."

Great. Talk about the proverbial needle in a haystack. What made Dad think we could ever find them? Did he expect to spot my glasses standing on the curb, holding a little suitcase, thumbing a ride? But since I was in no position to question anything, I found my way into the garage and into the passenger seat. Boy, there's nothing better for a hangover than a tense, blurry, silent car ride with your father.

"Well, do you see them?" he growled.

"How would I?" I shot back. I didn't mean to sound like a smart-ass, but from what I could make out of his face, I must've come across that way.

Suddenly, Dad jammed on the brakes, and without even bothering to pull the car to the side of the road, he grabbed my arm and led me to a group of bushes. As unbelievable as it sounds, there, sticking out right in the middle of some shrubs, were my glasses. It looked as though the Invisible Man was lurking in the bushes. One can only imagine what kind of odds Vegas would give for something like that.

As we drove home, I didn't even want to face my dad, especially since now I could actually see him, so I stared straight ahead. I didn't want to call any further attention to myself, so I didn't even bother to pull out the leaf that was stuck in the bridge of my spectacles. It must have looked like a bad attempt at camouflage. Finally, my father said, "I hope you've learned your lesson about alcohol."

This is another one of those moments that seem so

clear in retrospect. Had I been savvy enough, I might have taken this as a possible warning that maybe I'm one of those people who shouldn't drink. Alas, the only "lesson" I learned at that time was, always have a spare set of eyeglasses when you're out drinking.

Chapter

≋ **2** ≋

A Major in Comedy, Plus a Minor in Partying, Equals a BS in Relationships

When Rita and I broke up, my world was more shaken than a James Bond martini. I threw myself into reading all sorts of religious/spiritual books, searching for answers. My house is scattered with tomes such as *When Bad Things Happen to Good People*, *The Road Less Traveled*, *Conversations with God*, and *Chicken Soup for the Soul*. At one point, noting all these titles, my kindly housekeeper Anna asked me, "You okay, Mr. Ed?" I've always suspected that Anna knows more English than she likes to admit and fully realizes she's calling me the name of a talking horse. Anyway, she asked, "You okay, Mr. Ed?" and I said, "Yes, thank you, Anna; please dust off my copy of *Suicide for Dummies* and draw me a warm bath, won't you?"

Perhaps Rita and I were doomed from the start due

to our religious differences. I'm Catholic and she's Jewish, so that certainly created some problems. After all, it's two faiths that are deeply rooted in traditions — traditions that are often in direct opposition to one another. For instance, she didn't want a Christmas tree in the house. I didn't want a mezuzah in the house. And eventually, she didn't want *me* in the house.

She was always more spooked by my religion than I was by hers. I think she was unnerved during our arguments when I would sit staring at her, munching on communion wafers. She felt sheer terror imagining that our wedding ceremony might contain the "J" word and wasn't placated by my suggestion that as a compromise we could have the guests sing "Oy Vey Maria."

Relationships are probably the greatest showcase in the world for people's revisionist views. The friends who told me, "I always knew she was the perfect girl for you," are the same ones who after the breakup were saying, "I could always tell there was something off about her."

I can't begin to figure any of it out. All I know are two things: everyone has a different theory about relationships, and every one of those theories is wrong.

Oh, sure, there are some truths I've managed to distill, like the fact that relationships are about compromise. You tell your side, she tells her side, then you do what she says. It's about give and take. Your partner gives you shit, and you take it. Not to sound cynical.

Even when people are happy dating, at what point does it become clear that they should marry? I assume most couples get married when they've decided that they don't need to have sex anymore. There's a reason they call it "tying the knot."

People always say, "You'll know when it's the right one. You'll just know." To me, that's like showing up to work at a nuclear power factory having no previous experience.

"Say, what button do I push in case of disaster?"

"Oh, you'll know the right one. You'll just know."

It's nonsense. Everyone thinks they "know," or they wouldn't get married in the first place. I think it's why so many of my friends got married during college and ended up getting divorced before they even graduated. It's well known that many people attend college with the specific intention of meeting someone to marry. I, on the other hand, went to college for the proper reasons: to party and attend school sporting events.

⪴ ⪵

There was never any question that I would attend Ohio State University in Columbus. My sisters had all gone to college in Ohio as well, but none at State. Colleen went to Dayton, known for being the birthplace of the Wright Brothers; Maureen went to Ohio University, known for its partying; and Kathleen went to Kent State, known for, well, you know. My father, who graduated from Ohio State in 1942, had been taking me to football games there for as long as I could remember. Besides the spectacular stadium, known as The Horseshoe, I immediately fell in love with the entire campus. It's especially great in the fall when the plethora of trees turn various shades of orange, red, and yellow. Coincidentally, those are the same colors Coach Woody Hayes's face went through when a call went against his team.

My first day on campus, I saw a sign in the student union that advertised an "Amateur Comedy Contest." I decided I'd enter, and once again was the only person doing original material. It didn't seem fair to have to compete against the likes of George Carlin, Robert Klein, and Bill Cosby. Fortunately, those guys weren't there to actually deliver their material, so I managed to be crowned the winner. My favorite moment of the evening occurred when one student-performer, angry at the lack of response he was getting, whirled on the crowd and sputtered, "What's wrong with you fuckers? This here is some quality shit!" Amazingly, that bit of charm failed to win the audience over.

I won $25 and the immediate respect of my new roommates, who honored me by allowing me to spend all my winnings buying their beers for the night.

This was the early 1980s, and the so-called comedy boom was just beginning. That is, nightclubs that specialized in presenting stand-up comedy began to dot the landscape. One such establishment called "Giggles" had just opened in downtown Columbus. After much urging by my friends, I got the nerve to call up and inquire about performing on their open mic night. Naturally, I was so nervous I dialed the wrong number and went through the humiliation of asking, "Is this Giggles?" to some gravel-voiced stranger. He paused a moment, then said, "No, it's Tweety Bird, asshole!" and hung up on me.

When I finally got through to the real folks at Giggles, they told me to come down and sign up on Sunday night.

I trekked down to Giggles the next week, armed with my ten-minute routine consisting mostly of making fun of television commercials. I was accompanied by my roommates, who were hoping for a repeat of their evening of free beer. The backstage atmosphere was much more psychotic and competitive than at the student union. At nineteen, looking like I was twelve, I was clearly the youngest hopeful there. Most of the contestants were professional "open mikers," and I was awed as they told of their experiences performing in bars and other "real" clubs around central Ohio. A few were kind to me, that is, before I did well onstage. Most, however, were spooky and aloof, with a John Hinckley–like aura about them. I managed to win the contest that night as well. This time the prize was $50. My roommates immediately began popping Tylenol in anticipation of the alcohol to come.

A few weeks later, in my second try at Giggles, I won again, getting an even better response from the audience than I had the previous time. But most important, that night I was invited to open the professional shows the club featured Wednesday through Saturday.

My head was definitely in the clouds at that point. I could hardly sleep in the dorm, which wasn't unusual, since a college dorm has to be the noisiest place on the face of the earth. With our dorm, Steeb Hall, the good part was, there was always something happening. The bad part was, there was always something happening. That particular night, I was kept awake by the adrenaline of dreams of comedy greatness, which seemed within easy reach. I remember thinking, at this rate, I'm going to be a star within a year.

I got a nice, tall drink of cold reality just a few days later, on the Wednesday night of that very same week, during the first of the professional shows at which I was to perform. These audiences were different. Unlike the amateur night patrons who paid practically nothing to get in and were always on the lookout for somebody to root for among the large number of generally unfunny people, the folks at the "real" shows paid a lot of money and expected a lot of laughs in return. They weren't pulling for you. No, they expected you to prove that you're funny. The crowd was much smaller on Wednesday nights, probably about fifty, as opposed to the three hundred or so happy amateur night regulars. So even when a joke was well received, it didn't resonate nearly as well.

As a result of all of this, I got very nervous that night and pretty much bombed. There was no exit behind the stage, so after my set I had to walk through the crowd to get backstage. As I made my way off the stage that night, pale, sweaty, and wondering where I could score some cyanide, I heard some guy say to his date, "What the hell was *that?*"

I couldn't sleep in the dorm that night, either, but this time because I was tortured by nightmares of failure. What was I going to do for a living now? In my mind, I rehearsed the speech I would give the club owners, explaining that I'd never be coming back.

The next morning, I walked through campus all alone, then sat down to ponder my future over a cup of coffee at the student union, the very same place I'd won the student comedy competition. As I gazed at the stage where I'd been so successful just a few weeks earlier, the determination to pursue my dream began palpably surging through my veins. In retrospect, it might have just been the caffeine. I realized that my desire to perform comedy was greater than my fear of failure, even though it was a rather close race. A vaguely defiant confidence settled over my psyche.

That night, I returned to Giggles and took the stage as scheduled. Much to my relief, and surprise, I might add, I got huge laughs. I felt great afterward, once again encouraged that my dreams were within reach, but moreover, validated as a human being. Indeed, my psychological stability and emotional well-being rest entirely on my audience's reaction. This was the beginning of what would become a lifelong thought pattern of "I'm great," followed by "I'm shit," followed by "I'm great," followed by "I'm shit," followed by . . . you get the idea, depending on how I did onstage each night. A pretty healthy way to live for a mature human being, don't you think?

⋛ ⋚

I struggled to carry my old hot water heater out to the trash in the morning. LA is very serious about its garbage. Residents are supplied with various trash receptacles: one to hold glass, one for plastic, one for lawn clippings, one for solid waste, and one for papers. I bag each waste material separately, by category, careful to keep them apart; then I toss all the bags into my neighbor's yard while he's sleeping. Sometimes the pressure to properly categorize one's trash gets to be overwhelming. I mean, I'd hate to think that because I accidentally put an empty Yoo-hoo bottle in the "papers only" bin, I'm responsible for acid rain.

As I dropped my tank at the curb, a white car with a smiling man behind the wheel pulled into my driveway. I thought, *Hey, it's probably one of the neighbors I haven't met, just wanting to say "Hi."* Well, I was half right. He was one of my neighbors, only he was at my house in his official capacity as a city inspector. "Do you have a permit for that water heater?" he asked. "No, but I'm throwing it out anyway," I offered. "I assume you got a new one," he continued, "so should I assume you got a permit for the new one?" As it sank in that he was serious, the best I could blurt out was, "I didn't even know you had to have a permit," with a sick, Pee Wee Herman–like giggle. He eyed me with disdain. "Well, you do. You'll need to go to town hall today to get one."

My head was whirling. I've never heard of anyone in this town getting a permit for their water heater, but then I figured out why that is. Because the only way to get caught replacing a water tank without a permit is to have the inspector drive by the very six seconds you're dragging the old one to the curb. What are the odds? Pretty damn good if you're me.

The inspector introduced himself as Mark and told me he lived down the street. "I'll have to bring the wife by to meet you." *Great,* I thought, *she's probably with the IRS. She can sift through my tax records and he can write me a plumbing citation while I barbecue for them.* "I want to see that permit when I stop by later today," he said with an odd smile. For a brief moment, I entertained the thought of killing him and burying him in my backyard, but I realized I'd probably need a permit for that as well.

I shook my head in exasperation. It was amazing that no matter how black my mood already was, something always came along to make it even darker. If the black hole that was now my brain got any bigger, it might start absorbing asteroids and space station debris.

I tried to focus on the task that was directly in front of me, half-heartedly giving myself a pep talk. *Oh well,* I thought, *just go get the damn permit. Hey, how horrible could city hall be on a Saturday morning?*

Four hours in the packed, sweltering lobby later, after reading the same copy of "Penny-Pincher Shopper's Guide" for the fifteenth time (I would have done the crossword puzzle, but every line had been filled in with the word "shit," in ink), my number (two million four) was called to the "permits" window of city hall.

"I'd like a permit for my new hot water tank," I told the stern-looking woman in charge.

"You don't need a permit for a water tank, sir."

"That's not what my neighbor told me."

"Well, is your neighbor a city inspector?"

"As a matter of fact, he is."

"Are you sure?"

"I didn't see a badge or anything, but yeah, he seemed like one." Eventually, she had to make up a form by hand because apparently nobody had actually purchased a water tank permit in Los Angeles before, because the only way you could get caught is . . . well, you know. She wasn't even sure what to charge me, but twenty bucks seemed unreasonable enough, and I was out of there.

As I drove home, my resentment toward Mark the inspector began to fade as I realized that, in fact, it probably would behoove me to have him on my side. After all, with the amount of work I wanted to have done on my house, it might actually be a beneficial thing if I could curry some favor with an inspector. As long as I was on his good side, he might be able to help me out, perhaps cut through paperwork or give me hints on how to circumvent some of the more arcane city laws. Maybe he wasn't really such a stickler for the rules once someone got to know him. If he was even able to get me out of a parking ticket one time, it would be worth it.

I was surprised when I arrived home to find Inspector Mark waiting for me in front of my house. This time, though, I was ready for him. I bounded out of my car and waved my permit at him triumphantly. He was extremely pleased. "Hey, that's great; you got right on that. That shows me you respect the city, and that makes me respect you."

I felt like a little kid being praised for eating his vegetables.

"You know, I'm really on the homeowner's side," he continued. "People think I'm there to hassle them."

"I never thought that," I fibbed.

"In fact, I protect people from unscrupulous contractors," he offered.

"That must be a great feeling," I said, losing all respect for myself, yet determined to have a "friend" at city hall. "I'll bet you know all the important people in city government, huh? You probably get favors from powerful folks, like yourself, all the time."

"Well, I don't like to brag, Ed, but yeah, actually, I do."

"So," I asked, "did you come to see me for this permit? Or were you just making a social call? Do you want to come in for some coffee?"

"Actually, I just stopped over to say good-bye."

I gave him a puzzled look. "What do you mean?"

"I'm moving. Changing jobs. I'm going to San Diego to work in my brother's antique business."

I dropped my friendly visage. "So, checking this permit is basically your last official act?"

"Well, second to last. I'm afraid my very last official act is to give you this citation for improperly installed gutter spouts. Sorry." He tore off a $25 ticket and handed it to me. "But I'll take that coffee."

≷ ≷

My romantic situation wasn't any different in college than it had been in high school. I did go out with some nice coeds, but as usual, it would always end with someone getting hurt, and it all just depressed the hell out of me. At the age of twenty, I had already decided that the old adage "It is better to have loved and lost than to never have loved at all" was complete bullshit. It just couldn't have been more wrong. To begin with, I felt that if you didn't know what you were missing, then it wouldn't be a problem to miss it. As it was, I also felt that the downside of relationships—the hurt, the pain, the inconvenience, and the inevitable breakup—far outweighed any so-called positives that were to be gained. I mean, really, who wants companionship if you can have solitude? It's a feeling that stayed with me for a long, long time.

At the time, I was far more interested in making people laugh, goofing around, and hatching ridiculous pranks than I was in pursuing a relationship. Probably the favorite caper my roommates and I used to pull on people occurred whenever we'd hear someone in the dorm order a pizza. We'd immediately slip back to our room, call the pizza place our buddy had just ordered from, then, posing as that buddy, we'd completely change the order. Then we'd sit back and laugh at the chaos that ensued when a guy's extra-large with everything on it arrived as a small cheese sub.

Naturally, pizza is a big part of any college student's life, so it only figures it was involved in many of the stories I remember from those years. It seems that whenever I get together with old college chums, 95 percent of the stories begin with the words, "Remember the time when we were really drunk and ordered a pizza and . . ."

That being said, I remember the time when we were really drunk and ordered a pizza and went down to the lobby to meet the delivery guy. Since the meal at the commons had been tuna soufflé that evening, it was no surprise that someone else had ordered at the same time as my roommate, Carl, and I had. Our delivery man walked in with two pizzas and started checking to see which was ours. He suddenly remembered he had left our Pepsi back in his car and handed us both boxes when he left to retrieve the soda. Big mistake! After identifying our pizza, Carl opened the other box and took a huge bite out of the pie, barely closing the box and slurping the cheese off his beard as the delivery man reappeared with our Pepsi. As we were paying him, two girls came down and paid for their order, the one that Carl had sampled. They didn't open their box before paying, and they got into the same elevator as we did. We couldn't even look at them, knowing what ghastly surprise awaited them when they sat down to eat.

"Mmm, it smells good," said one girl.

"I'll bet it looks good," offered Carl. He opened our box, gazed lovingly at our pie, and nodded with satisfaction. This had the intended effect of causing the girls to open their box, and when they saw the huge bite taken out of their pizza, they both let out a scream like Janet Leigh showering at the Bates Motel.

⸙ ⸙

I worked hard at decorating my house. It struck me that the only difference in the decor of my bedroom now from my bedroom at thirteen is that now all my sports posters are framed. And since it's *my* house, *every* room has framed sports posters. Instead of tacking the cover of *Sports Illustrated* featuring John Havlicek up on my wall, I hang a framed *SI* cover featuring John Havlicek, signed by John Havlicek, up on my wall. I would hang John Havlicek himself up on my wall if he ever became available on eBay. When Billy Crystal showed me a seat from Yankee stadium autographed to him by Mickey Mantle, I wanted to weep. Who says guys aren't in touch with their feelings?

This sort of sports zealotry might seem rather disturbing to some, but know this: there are a lot of people like me out there. We're just hard-working folks who use sports as an outlet. You see these guys at ball games in strange costumes with these elaborate, hand-painted banners and you wonder, when do they find the time to design and make these outfits and signs? The answer is, during the time that they're supposed to be tightening a critical bolt in your car engine.

The two greatest inventions ever devised for the relocated sports addict are the satellite dish and the VCR. Some people can't enjoy a game unless it's live, a viewpoint I don't quite understand. It's like saying you can't enjoy a movie unless you watch it as it's being filmed. If I'm watching it on tape and don't know the result, then it's live.

If I've taped a ball game and I come home and see

that I have messages on my answering machine, I absolutely will not check them. I don't want to take the risk of someone blurting out the score on the machine before I have a chance to view it. Avoiding the results before watching a game on tape can be trickier than many people realize. I often feel as if the gods enjoy finding new ways to inform me of a score I'm trying to avoid.

A classic example is one night when I was performing at the Funnybone in Pittsburgh, back at the beginning of my career. I was doing three shows on a Saturday night, so I taped that evening's Pirates–Phillies game. I was really looking forward to relaxing at home while watching the tape. I kept the radio off in my car, and as I got to my apartment around 2 a.m. and was keying in the door, I felt very pleased that I had made it home still ignorant of the score. Just then, a neighbor I'd never seen before and never would see again arrived and began keying into his apartment, two doors down from mine. I nodded politely, and before I could get inside he said, "Hi, how's it going? I was at the Pirates game tonight; they scored five runs in the last inning to pull it out. Are you a fan?" He seemed surprised when I gave him a look like he'd just told me he'd run over my dog. I mumbled, "Yeah, I *was* a fan," then staggered into my apartment as if I'd been smashed over the head with a shovel. I think I'd have preferred that to having my game ruined.

So, in order to give myself the best opportunity to not know an outcome prematurely, I'll only retrieve my phone calls after viewing the game. This often isn't until hours later.

I realize this is a bit over the top, even by my standards. It used to bug Rita to no end, because she'd sometimes leave me a message she felt was important, knowing damn well I might not hear it for quite a while because I was protecting my opportunity to watch a game on tape. She always said, "God forbid there should be an emergency call." She had a point. I can just picture myself on the phone the next morning: "Sorry to hear you fell down last night, Grandma; I just got your message this morning. If you're still lying there, I can come over and help you up now." Fortunately, nothing like that has actually ever happened.

Of course, I realize that my sports fanaticism may be yet another obstacle to having a meaningful relationship with a woman. It's not easy to find a female who shares my consuming passion for sports. Of course, she doesn't have to be a *huge* fan, just as long as she doesn't mind *me* being one. It works for my parents. My father is a huge sports fan. My mom finds sports somewhat compelling, but she's certainly not in Dad's league. The important thing is that she's tolerant of his fanaticism, though she usually ends up going to the farthest corner of the house when my dad and I are watching a big game, screaming at the TV.

One of my favorite moments was when my father was moaning over a game between two teams he really didn't even have a connection to, cursing the officials, the coaches, the fans, and the vendors. Dad finally shouted, "This is horrible, I can't stand it!" and my mother offered, "If you're going to get so upset, why don't you turn it off?" My father snapped, "Let me enjoy myself, goddammit!"

I completely understand such behavior, though many others, such as Rita, definitely do not. And I'll admit that I do see a downside to sports, a personal one that others can't possibly see. For me, it's when I interpret things that happen to one of my teams as a reflection of what my life is about. As absurd as it is to take sporting events personally that I'm not even participating in, I can read lots of things into the most innocent events. My team fumbles on the opponent's goal line, and I see it as an indication that I will get close to some career goal but won't be lucky enough to attain it. My team loses a game it's heavily favored to win, and I'm reminded of times when I've underachieved. My team loses in heartbreaking fashion, and I feel it's indicative of the heartbreak I've suffered and will continue to suffer on stage and off, regardless of what I deserve. This is when my sports fanaticism gets a bit twisted. The constructive outlet of emotions turns into a destructive omen of my professional and personal favors. I realize it's ironic that though I'm aware being a fan will invariably bring me pain at times, I'm still willing to invest emotionally in sports, while even the remote possibility of pain in a relationship with a woman makes me shy away from them altogether.

⇒ ⇐

I really hated leaving Ohio State. But every fiber of my being told me that the time had arrived to pursue a full-time career in comedy. And after all, by my junior year, I had pretty much lost interest in my studies, as my grade point average readily indicated. Actually, I had been thinking strongly for quite some time about leaving school, or at least taking a hiatus, but I certainly wasn't going to leave before fall quarter, not with a home football slate of UCLA, Wisconsin, and Michigan. However, once January of my junior year rolled around, I faced the fact that all I really cared about was performing at local clubs. And when I wasn't doing that, I spent the rest of my time writing and distributing *Hoseheadlines*, a satirical paper detailing the exploits of our dorm residents. A typical issue contained such newsworthy items as:

- At dinner, Mike Kope found a worm in his potato and showed it to the head of the commons. Her reply? "Don't worry about it honey; it's already paid for in your fees."
- Ken Chance ran into some trouble at the Valentine's Day party when he interpreted a drink thrown in his face as a "yes" to his request for a slow dance.
- The rumor that Scott Everett actually passed his astronomy exam last week was vehemently denied by both Scott and his deeply chagrined parents.

Not exactly the stuff of *National Lampoon*, but an enjoyable creative outlet for me nonetheless. Still, I felt it was time to move on.

Everything seemed to be pointing me toward grabbing for the proverbial brass ring. As they say, that first step is a doozy, but I took it, by leaving school. At the time, I fully intended to go back and get my degree sometime in the future. After all, a diploma is the ultimate Ohio State souvenir. Well, maybe second to one of those scarlet and gray beer hats.

Understandably, my folks were less than thrilled with this decision. It wasn't exactly their dream to have their child announce he was leaving school to become a comedian. It probably would have sounded better to them if I said I was quitting in order to join a cult. I suppose in a way, I was. But even though they had their doubts and concerns, my parents gave me both moral and, especially at the beginning, financial support. I even moved back in with them. I made a deal with Mom and Dad, essentially that I'd give comedy a try for a year or so, and if it didn't work out, I'd go back to school. Suffice it to say, I do not have a college degree.

A lot of my friends gave me credit for "being so courageous," which at times I took as an insult. I thought, *Hey, they must not think I'm very talented, if they see it as such a brave thing.* It was hard for me to realize that they were merely recognizing the slim odds of anyone, no matter how talented, achieving the sort of success in the entertainment business I was after. This is a perfect example of my very peculiar interpretive skills: I often take something that's meant as a compliment as a criticism. To this day, if, for example, I hand in three sketches to a network and the producer says, "Hey, I read your material and I especially loved the one about golf," my immediate question is, "So, you didn't like the other two sketches?"

As for quitting school to do comedy, well, I suppose it did take guts to pursue my dream. But in all honesty, I felt confident in my abilities, and that confidence was further spurred by the modest success I had already experienced. Certainly, a healthy dose of naïveté was added to the equation, because in my heart, I felt destined to be successful. I wasn't contemplative enough to realize that most people who've tried and failed had probably felt that way, too. I considered it a birthright to achieve my goals in comedy. This sense of entitlement worked in my favor particularly in the beginning, emboldening me to push forward in show business. But eventually my sense of entitlement entitled me to nothing but unhappiness.

Chapter

⋟3⋞

Up My Career

After moving back to Pittsburgh, I began to work regularly at a club called the Funnybone. I was hired by the owners, two well-meaning but constantly bickering brothers. In a dynamic that one could easily see had been playing out all their lives, they'd get into some incredibly nasty verbal spats and were never shy about doing it in front of employees and customers alike. I distinctly remember one brother snapping at the other, "Hey, eat my shit!" in front of a group of stunned patrons. During shows, they'd often slip into the kitchen area to "discuss" something, and from onstage I could hear them shouting at each other. Periodically, they'd poke their heads out into the showroom, make sure people were laughing, then go back into the kitchen and continue arguing. Ah, the world of "professional" show business.

I was lucky enough to work with a wide assortment of great comedic talent. People such as Jay Leno, Paul Reiser, Steven Wright, and Dennis Miller came through regularly. Miller is a native of Pittsburgh and by that time was established as the big fish in the city. I was in awe of his command of the language as well as how extremely prolific he was. He was nice enough to give me compliments and advice in the early stages of my career, and his encouragement was especially heartening when I watched him progress to New York City, *Saturday Night Live,* and stardom.

Now that I was doing comedy professionally, I was constantly under pressure to create new material. A common question asked of me and other comedians is, "Where do you get your ideas?" For some reason, that's how people always refer to it. It's never "your jokes," or "your stories," or "your humor," it's always "your ideas," as if I'm Thomas Edison. Often, I'll say, "I purchase my ideas at an idea store downtown. In fact, just this morning I bought the idea for the answer I just gave you to your question."

In reality, I guess I shouldn't expect people to know that my ideas come from everywhere, everybody, and everything. For whatever reason, my mind has always worked this way, viewing just about everything that happens in life as a possible joke, or a possible sketch, or a possible scene for a movie.

Why is this? Who knows? I guess it's the same reason that some people can look at a sunset and write a song about it, or some people can take a lump of clay and mold it into a beautiful sculpture. I can't do either of those things, so to me it's mind-boggling that others can, but to those who can write music or sculpt, it's completely intuitive and probably hard for them to understand why anyone *can't* do it. It's the same kind of thing for me and comedy. I believe absolutely everyone has their own singular abilities that enable them to perform certain tasks fairly effortlessly, tasks that others find almost impossible to execute. These are the gifts that make us all unique.

Other humans I interact with often are comedy guinea pigs without knowing it. When I'm in a social situation, though I'm not purposely "trying out" material on people, I often will say something during the normal course of the conversation that makes them laugh. I usually make a mental note of it for possible use later. Ideally, I write the thought down before it disappears, which, with my short-term memory, is often the second it comes out of my mouth.

Unless I'm with close friends, I won't write anything down in front of people. I don't want folks to suddenly feel like they're at a function at Bob Woodward's house.

I keep a notebook and pencil in my car, and pens and legal pads are scattered about my house, for those times when inspiration hits. Yet somehow, whenever I need a pen to write down an important phone number, none can be found.

I sometimes will dictate thoughts into a little tape recorder, but I discovered that one has to be careful with that method. On one occasion, while talking with people at a party, I said something I thought could be useful for my routine. I excused myself from the living room and went into the bathroom to record my thoughts. I had to pee as well, so I multitasked and did both simultaneously. Unfortunately, I hadn't locked the door, and another guest barged right into the john. Though I was stunned, the intruder was even more surprised to see me standing there, whizzing while talking into a tape recorder. It was quite embarrassing for both of us. The best I could do was turn to him and say, "Uh, I like to keep a journal of what my urine looks like each time I go. That's why they call this machine a 'dick-taphone.'" A moment that scarred us both for life, I'm sure.

Sometimes a friend will say something that's really funny and I'll laugh and want to use it in my work. In keeping with my belief in not stealing other people's thoughts, I'll always ask if I can use the remark. Usually, they're excited about that idea and will tell their friends about it. Until, of course, they see me bomb onstage with the remark. Then they point out rather quickly how it was funny when they said it, but I had somehow screwed it up.

By 1987, my stand-up had garnered me a lot of attention in Pittsburgh, and I was hired to do segments on the local CBS affiliate, KDKA-TV. The station had an afternoon show called *Pittsburgh 2Day* (because it was on channel 2, you see) and I would appear with prop-oriented bits, such as wacky gift suggestions for the holidays or bogus cooking segments. The audience for the show, both in-studio and at home, was mostly house-wives, so I had to somewhat dial back my penchant for edgy humor.

My best memory was getting to live out a fantasy when I shot a remote video segment about the opening day of the baseball season. I got to put on a Pirates uniform and run around the turf at Three Rivers Stadium, this time without being chased out by security.

My worst memory is one afternoon when I was scheduled to appear on the show to present souvenirs I'd supposedly collected at Graceland. It was the week of Elvis's birthday, and right before I went on, the host, a lovely, talented, and kind woman named Patrice King Brown, pulled me aside. "I have to warn you," she whispered. "The whole audience is stacked with women from the Southwestern Pennsylvania Elvis Presley Fan Club. What kind of jokes are you planning to do?"

"Uh-oh," I replied. I had ten minutes of jokes like, "Do you know why they called him the King? It was short for Burger King," and "Do you know what TCB stood for? Twenty Cheeseburgers." I also had a slew of equally offensive props, such as Elvis's girdle and a guitar-shaped pill box.

I was feeling sick to my stomach, but since it was a live show, I had little choice but to go on and wing it as best I could. Fortunately, I was able to adjust on the fly, explaining on air that I didn't have any props from Graceland because the guards didn't like how I looked and wouldn't let me in. I ended up mostly making fun of myself for not being able to gain access to a tourist attraction that literally millions have no problem visiting regularly. I wrapped up my segment by giving an impassioned speech about how Elvis should be on a postage stamp. The audience roared their approval, and I could barely see Patrice smiling at me since we were both so covered in bullshit.

At that same time, I started doing radio ads for the Pittsburgh Pirates, then got the opportunity to go to spring training to film a series of television commercials promoting the upcoming season. Needless to say, I was very excited. I had always dreamed of going to spring training, and now I got to go and get paid, too. The Pirates train in Bradenton, Florida, in a tremendous little park called McKechnie Field. I shot the commercials in the morning, then watched games in the afternoon. Everybody should have such a schedule.

I did spots with manager Jim Leyland, second baseman Johnny Ray, and first baseman Sid Bream. Believe me, if I had known back then in 1987 that Bream, as a Brave in 1992, would go on to score the most devastating run against the Pirates in franchise history, I'd have taken out his knee right there, à la Tonya Harding/Nancy Kerrigan.

The whole experience was a total blast, in many ways. Baseball people and advertising executives were fun folks to hang out with, because when I compared myself to them, I didn't feel like I really drank all that much.

Just a few days before the TV spots were due to begin airing, the publicity folks at the Pirates decided to pull all the ads because they were "too silly." This was a team that had just lost one hundred games, and they didn't want to be embarrassed by me? It certainly wouldn't be the last time the phrase *bitter disappointment* was to be connected with my experiences in show business. Or with my personal affairs, for that matter.

Being somewhat in the local public eye did allow me to meet women, but, as usual, I held them at arm's length. Conveniently, my lifestyle of traveling and working odd hours was a perfect excuse to avoid engaging in a serious relationship. For a while I dated Annie, a waitress at the Funnybone, but it seemed mostly out of convenience for both of us. Interestingly, Paul Reiser also started dating one of the Funnybone waitresses, a really sweet girl named Paula, and they are actually married today and have a lovely family. Certainly, this was an incredible exception to the usual comic/waitress liaison.

Although Annie and I had genuine affection for one another, we also were two young, insecure people who seemed to have a constant need to make each other jealous. She would flirt with other comics, and I would flirt with other waitresses or with women from the audience. Though it was just the sort of depressing gamesmanship that kept me feeling so cynical about relationships, at the time it seemed to be an inevitable and necessary part of any romantic liaison.

Naturally, since I drew on everyday happenings for my routines, my real-life experiences with others often aired publicly. This created some resentment, especially when what aired publicly was a private relationship. And when I was doing the jokes in the very club where the person I had the relationship with was working, life and art overlapped in an inexcusable way. Not that I'd ever use somebody's real name, but it wasn't the most comfortable of situations for Annie. Oops.

It became clear that the meaning and significance of comedy in my life had steadily evolved over time. What had started out as a lark, a way of having fun in grade school, had morphed into a way to protect myself from emotional harm and to become popular in high school. Needless to say, I wasn't always successful. In college, humor developed into an instrument of ambition, enabling me to make a name for myself and giving me the confidence to abandon the traditional route of education as a way of launching a career. I often wondered whether I was out of my mind. And when I finally went from amateur to professional, I began to appreciate the limitless possibilities of comedy as a tool for dealing with life. The jury is still out on whether this is a sign of my growing maturity as a person, or whether it proves that I just don't want to grow up.

Usually, performing was a cathartic experience. Sometimes, it was a release from pent-up resentments. At other times, it became a way to talk about my fears, and thus render them less potent. At still other times, stand-up was a great way to vent a passionately held opinion and attempt to sway other's opinions through humor. Of course, at times, doing comedy meant nothing other than being funny for the sake of being funny.

The edge to my humor definitely puts some people off. Many folks along the way have thought that I was especially bitter, or angry, when I wasn't really. Fortunately, most people who get to really know me understand that much of my dark sarcasm is merely a part of my job. But not everyone understands that. Annie certainly didn't, and predictably she and I split up. She was bothered by the fact that I occasionally talked about "us" onstage. While her feelings of discomfiture were regrettable, using my life experiences to fuel my comedy was absolutely necessary. It was, and still is, an integral part of who I am as a performer, and breaking up with her was a predictable consequence I was all too willing to accept. I hadn't done anything to purposely embarrass her, so my conscience was clear. If she couldn't handle this part of me, so be it. Strange how my sense of humor often attracts women to me and then, ultimately, turns into a chief catalyst in driving them away.

Though I missed spending time with Annie, any feelings of regret I might have allowed myself were pushed to the side. I was too busy touring around the country to waste any time on sentimental thoughts.

I was performing in a club in San Antonio, Texas, one week when Henny Youngman dropped by the club. He was doing a show at the local arena and just came by to do a quick guest performance. As it turned out, it was right before I was scheduled to go on.

The startled crowd gave him a huge ovation when he hit the stage, and he proceeded to wow us all with fifteen minutes of classic material. Though he was well into his late seventies by that time, he delivered his lines flawlessly.

My joy in watching him quickly turned into fear about performing after him. I took the stage and said, "Wow, nobody will ever believe this. Henny Youngman was my opening act." Henny laughed sympathetically, as did the audience, and much to my relief, I went on to have a very good show.

I spoke to him briefly afterward, and he was extremely gracious and friendly. I wished him well at his engagement over the weekend and headed back to my hotel.

I was more than surprised when the phone rang early the next morning in my hotel room. Groggily picking up the receiver, I heard "Hello, Ed?"

"Uh, yeah."

"This is Henny Youngman. How'd you like to have breakfast with me?"

"Uh, of course. It would be an honor, Mr. Youngman."

"Call me Henny."

"Yes, sir."

"That doesn't sound like 'Henny'—that sounds like 'sir.'"

"Yes sir, uh, Henny."

"Meet me down in the lobby in twenty minutes."

It turned out that Mr. Youngman, I mean Henny, was staying at the same hotel as I. I dressed quickly and raced downstairs to meet him. We had a leisurely breakfast, and I was fascinated to hear so many great stories from a genuine living legend. Besides being hilarious, he was also an extremely sweet person.

It happened to be Mother's Day, and he confided that his beloved wife of many years had died on Mother's Day the year before. I listened with interest and compassion as he expounded at length on the wonderful relationship he'd shared with his wife. Despite his signature line of "Take my wife—please," he described her as a source of support and inspiration that made his life worth living. Certainly food for thought for me. I held the belief that women and relationships were more likely obstacles to success, and here was Henny basically telling me that a good relationship was integral to success not only in comedy, but in life as well. Ultimately, I found the idea of such closeness with and dependency on another person so uncomfortable that I chose to keep my blinders on and race toward my goals, superficial as they now seem in retrospect. Unfortunately, I didn't have the capacity to grasp Henny's wisdom at that point in my life.

Henny and I ended up going to the biggest tourist attraction San Antonio is known for: the Alamo. As we entered, he said loudly, "Hey, I forgot the Alamo." People were stunned to turn around and see Henny Youngman saying this. We were mobbed as we walked around the site, and Henny kept repeating his "I forgot the Alamo" line to the delight of everyone.

As people fussed over him and he signed autographs,

he'd always point to me and tell them, "This is a really funny guy, too." His efforts to make me feel included were appreciated, and still are. Just a very nice man.

As we said our good-byes later that evening, he produced a copy of one of the many joke books he'd written and signed it for me. It's one of my most prized possessions.

Later that same year, I got the chance to open for Sheena Easton at several amphitheaters in upper New York State. The shows were nerve wracking, because I'd never been in front of a live crowd bigger than five hundred before. The audiences for my shows up there were anywhere between five and twenty *thousand* people. All I could think beforehand was *Man, if that many people think I suck, they sure could make some noise about it.* The night before the first show, I had an incredibly vivid dream. I took the stage before Sheena and was heckled and booed mercilessly. I could see every detail of the angry faces in the front row. I woke up soaked in cold sweat. Not exactly the kind of experience that calms one down before a show.

I didn't tell anyone about my dream, logically determining that if I did, it would come true. That night at the Saratoga Springs amphitheater, I stood backstage, peeking out from behind the curtain as the crowd settled in. Honest to God, if I had seen any of those faces from my dream, I would not have gone on. When the stage manager came up behind me and put his hand on my shoulder, I almost vaulted into the tenth row.

"Wow, I guess you're a little jumpy, huh?" he laughed. He didn't know the half of it.

Fortunately, the crowd was very receptive, and as the laughs washed over me like a comforting summer breeze, I began to relax and actually enjoy myself. I used a little mental trick to focus. (No, not imagining people in their underwear.) I concentrated on only the first few rows of the audience, pretending they were the only people there. It worked. The only time I got nervous was when my mind started to drift and I began to look at the upper decks and realized how many people were listening to me. My leg literally began to shake. I snapped myself out of it and went back to concentrating on only the first few rows.

And so, despite my nightmare the previous evening that I feared was a premonition, the whole experience was terrific. As was so often, but not always, the case, my fear was completely unfounded.

While success was becoming a part of my life then, fear was steadily becoming an even bigger part. Just what fears did I have? I suppose an easier question would be, just what fears didn't I have? I had fear of getting too close to a woman. Fear of not getting too close to a woman. Fear of losing my success. Fear of not getting what I wanted. Fear of actually getting what I wanted. Fear of contradictory fears! I was afraid I wouldn't get the breaks I deserved, or that I'd get those breaks but then something terrible would happen, such as an accident or the contraction of some incurable disease. I started getting depressed when I realized how long my list of fears was, which of course then added the fear of being depressed.

Though alcohol helped deaden a lot of these anxieties on a temporary basis, they were always there waiting for me when I sobered up. Friends tried to help me, telling me that "F-E-A-R" merely stood for "False Evidence Appearing Real." But my concern was, what if it really stood for "Fuck Ed At Random"?

Chapter

$\gtrless 4 \lessgtr$

Bombed in Boston

O ne of the side benefits of a broken engagement, other than the general embarrassment
and emotional scarring for life, is dealing with
the engagement ring. You guys thought it was a hassle
buying it? Try returning it after a breakup. I imagine it
would be easier to return a kidney transplant, and as I
came to find out, far less painful.

When I first began shopping for Rita's ring, I was, of
course, horrified to find out the cost of diamonds, or
rather, what they charge for diamonds. I thought the
markup on pizza was high. At least with pizza the plea-
sure lasts for a while. I love all the diamond ads in maga-
zines asking, "Isn't she worth two months' salary?" What
they neglect to mention is that they want you to pay two
months of Bill Gates's salary. And if they really are talking
about two months of my salary, well, I work freelance, so

the question becomes, which two months? How about the two I was on unemployment?

I got to learn all about the diamond "Cs": color, clarity, carat, can't afford it. I haven't seen that many expensive Cs since George W. Bush's Yale transcript. Blinded by horrifically bad judgment disguising itself as "love," I ended up purchasing the ring of her dreams (and my nightmares) for a "discount" of $20,000. The whole time I was thinking, *Hell, for $20,000, it should be Joe Montana's Super Bowl ring.*

She enjoyed showing off the ring to her friends, and I was happy to see her do so, though in my mind the perspective was a bit different. When I looked at the ring, I didn't see a diamond. I saw the home entertainment system for my den that I didn't have.

At least it wasn't hard to get the ring back from Rita. (And I had no idea she could throw that hard.) After our relationship ended, I decided that I needed to get rid of the ring as fast as possible. I had enough hurtful reminders around. I didn't need one that could cut glass.

Some friends suggested that I keep it in a safe deposit box and give it to *the next woman I get engaged to,* which to me was like saying, "Why don't you save that Sebuku sword for your *next* suicide?" Besides, I couldn't stand to give a ring with that history to another woman. Even if she didn't know, I would. Talk about inviting bad karma. I might as well give my next intended bride a mirror that I broke while ducking under a ladder to avoid a black cat that had knocked over my salt shaker. No, I wanted this evil talisman out of my life for good.

I called Ahmos Hassan, a good friend who also happens to be my manager, or "babysitter," as he likes to joke. (I think he's joking.) I told him I was returning the ring to the Beverly Hills store where I'd bought it and that if he'd go with me, I'd use some of the money I received to take us out for a nice, expensive meal. He readily agreed, but warned me that I probably wouldn't get back what I'd paid for the ring. I told him I realized that and that I'd be happy with $15,000 or so. Fortunately, I didn't really need the dough, but I wanted to get it and spend it on cool stuff for myself to try to feel better about the whole disaster. Maybe I'd give some of the funds to charity, too. Perhaps I'd even start one, "Ring Purchase Survivors," or something like that.

I drove to Ahmos's office in Century City, navigating the usual brutal LA traffic, made all the more unpleasant by ubiquitous SUVs. Somehow, people are sold this notion that SUVs are safer than other cars. Perhaps, but certainly not for the other cars the SUVs plow into. Plus, SUVs roll over more often than France in world wars. If SUV dealers really want to showcase their product in a realistic environment, they should start displaying these vehicles overturned on their roofs, on fire. I can hear the salesman now, "Hey, want to take it out for a test-crash?"

I finally met up with Ahmos, and we entered "Quality Carats," the Beverly Hills establishment that was the scene of the crime, and asked to speak with the folks in charge. The management was all smiles until I said I wanted to return my jewelry. Their practiced grins disappeared faster than pastry in Pavarotti's dressing room. I explained my situation and told them I didn't want it anymore. I admitted that I knew they couldn't refund my money, but I just wanted some dough back. They could sell it to the next sap, er, man in love.

The store manager, a fellow named Ron, actually asked me, "Well, what happened with you two?" As if he was some concerned relative. I was tempted to blurt out something equally inappropriate, like "Well, Ron, I just couldn't get an erection with her anymore, you know?" but I managed to maintain a small amount of dignity. Ron commented that they don't normally buy jewelry. I said, "Neither do I." Ron told me he understood and asked if perhaps I'd like to trade the ring in for some other merchandise. I said, "Yes, where are your big screen televisions?" He looked at me for a moment, then excused himself to take the ring into the back room to "determine its worth."

"According to my ex, it's worth nothing," I joked bitterly as he turned his back and scurried off.

As Ahmos and I wandered uneasily about the store, I saw the sales clerk I had dealt with all those months ago. I gave her an awkward wave. At first she smiled; then it hit her. She remembered who I was, and when she realized that I was attempting to make a return, she suddenly turned her head away as if she'd just spotted an old gym teacher who'd made unwanted advances in the sixth-grade locker room.

After what seemed an eternity, Ron came back and said, "It's a beautiful ring. How much did you pay for it?" "Twenty grand," I replied. "Impossible," he shot back. "But I bought it from *you* guys; I have the receipt!" I pulled out the dog-eared piece of paper I'd been carrying around in my pocket for self-flagellation purposes. "Hey, ask her! She sold it to me!" I pointed to the sales lady, who at that juncture literally somersaulted into the back room. Ron looked at the receipt and said, "Well, yes, I see it's insured for $20,000, but, you know, there's a bit of a markup and all." He was becoming visibly nervous at this point. "Fine," I said. "Then what can you offer me?" I had been naive enough to assume that a diamond was always worth what it was worth, but I was about to learn the truth, the hard way. He giggled uncomfortably and said, "Probably about $5,000."

After the smelling salts kicked in, I got up from the floor and asked him why he could only give me one fourth what I'd paid. Somehow the ring devalued $15,000 while it was on Rita's finger. Ron basically admitted that they'd ripped me off, but tried to assuage me by saying the diamond industry rips *everybody* off. He also admitted that they could resell my ring for $20,000 to someone else, but that *he* could never pay that much for it. "Yeah, you wouldn't want to be so stupid," I muttered. He suggested that we visit two other stores right there in Beverly Hills that "specialized" in purchasing "pre-owned" gems. He told us he was sure we could do much better at one of those places, and wrote down the addresses of both establishments on the back of my receipt. "Tell them Ron sent you," he advised.

"Oh, I will," I said. "Clearly, you're the man with clout." Ron looked relieved as he watched us exit.

We entered the first store he'd suggested and were immediately set upon by the classic snooty saleswoman. Though Ahmos and I were both dressed nicely, she eyed us as if we were two indigents who'd just stopped by to steal some toilet paper. I explained, "Ron sent us. He said you might want to buy this ring."

"We don't buy; we only sell!!" she snapped. Gee, thanks for the lead, Ron. We left and headed for store number two.

Walking into this place was like suddenly stepping into a basement in Morocco, circa 1934. We were greeted by a suspicious-looking guy in a three-piece suit, whose air of dishonesty was overpowered only by the cologne that he had apparently flushed through every available pore. "May I help you?" he sneered. "Uh, yeah," I replied, eyeing the strange artifacts on the shelves. "Can I buy some Gremlins here?" After I explained my situation in more detail than I cared to, the Cologne Man gruffly produced a jeweler's loupe and began examining the ring. "That's a big contact lens," I joked weakly. He refused to look at me, which I considered almost payment enough in itself.

As he studied the gem carefully, Ahmos and I scanned the store and noticed that one of the sales clerks looked just like George Hamilton. This turned out to be because it was George Hamilton. Just in case this whole scene wasn't surreal enough, the always-tanned star of

Evel Knievel, Dynasty, and most recently, *The George and Alana Show,* was making small talk with the other staffers. "My God, what's this about?" Ahmos whispered. "Do you think he works here?" I asked Cologne Man if that was indeed George Hamilton, and he grunted in the affirmative, still not taking his eye off the gem. "Uh, is he for sale?" I asked.

After George's boys offered us $4,000 for a ring they would then turn around and sell for $20,000, we told them "no deal" and left. George walked out right when we did, calling out to the staff, "See you tomorrow, guys." Maybe he *did* work there.

Ultimately, I went back to see Ron, and I settled for $6,000 in return for the ring. He should have worn a condom for that transaction. He also guaranteed me a $4,000 credit for my next jewelry purchase at his store. Yeah, I'll tuck that into my wallet, right next to my "hell freezes over" coupon.

≳ ≲

By 1990, I felt that I'd done as much as I could for my career in Pittsburgh. Since I had no romantic connection tethering me there, I packed up and moved to Boston. I had been playing clubs there regularly, and the comedy scene was really vibrant at that time. Also, there are so many colleges and universities in the New England area that it was possible to make a living just performing on that circuit.

I was fortunate enough to fall in with a bright,

inventive, and fun group of comics who called Catch A Rising Star, in Cambridge, their home. It was a great room, located at the bottom of a steep set of stairs, in a giant basement right in the heart of Harvard Square. Unlike a lot of the other clubs and bars we performed in, the crowds there were not only receptive to, but actually encouraging of, bright material. You always felt that you could take a risk and try out some more esoteric things. If it didn't get a laugh, at least nobody got angry at you. Unlike some clubs where people seemed irritated that anyone would have the temerity to try and entertain them, the patrons of Catch A Rising Star always seemed to appreciate your effort.

I became a writer/performer in a sketch troupe called Cross Comedy. It was headed by David Cross, one of the inventive stars of HBO's *Mr. Show* and FOX's *Arrested Development.* Not that we were immodest, but we always felt we were a talented bunch. Time has actually borne that out, as most of us have gone on to have successful careers in the entertainment industry. In addition to David and myself, Jonathan Groff went on to become head writer for *Late Night with Conan O'Brien,* Lauren Dombrowski a producer on *MADtv,* John Ennis appeared regularly on shows like *Frasier,* and John Benjamin does voices on *Dr. Katz.* Guest performers included people such as Janeane Garofalo, Lewis Black, and Louie CK. The irony is that it seems we had to split up in order to be truly successful.

While Cross Comedy had many inspired triumphs, we also had some really spectacular failures. These pieces, too numerous and embarrassing to mention (and many written by me), ended up offending just about everyone, including ourselves.

Cross Comedy did enjoy a cult following, but then, so did David Koresh. While the audiences and critics in the Boston area were kind to us, it seemed that whenever producers from LA or New York came to scout us, something terrible would happen. Such as when, during a show in front of possible investors, John Ennis threw a fake punch that was too convincing, because the punch actually landed on Jim DeCroteau's nose. The laughter stopped immediately as Jim's blood flew around the stage as if someone had blown up a Red Cross lab. As luck would have it, Jim was in the next sketch, too, and gamely stayed onstage bleeding into a handkerchief as he assumed the role of a father driving his family to their vacation spot. The audience was completely freaked out, and once again, fate had intervened to prevent us from going beyond our little New England orbit.

By 1993, a lot of the comedy clubs in New England began to struggle financially. This was due to a combination of mismanagement, market saturation, and good old-fashioned stupidity. Many clubs closed completely. As the market began to dry up, I realized that I'd better diversify my resume if I wanted to continue to enjoy the high-living perks I'd grown accustomed to, such as eating. I noticed a help-wanted ad in the *Boston Globe* for "humor writers." I called the number and found out that it was a local greeting card manufacturer, a small outfit that was looking for someone to fax in jokes. I thought,

Great, I'm clearly their guy; as someone who's made a living for years writing humor, I'm probably overqualified for this little gig. I wrote about five pages of quick one-liners and confidently sent them off. About a week later, I received a letter informing me that my work wasn't "funny or original enough." I felt like I'd just been told by Burger King that I was unqualified to clean the grill.

In addition to my comedic pursuits, I formed a guitar/ singing duet—called Old School, Sir—with my friend Dana Thurston. The name was inspired by a drunken stranger we'd met at a local sports tavern, who'd counter any praise we gave to a modern ballplayer by simply mumbling, "Old school, sir. Old school."

Though I began playing music in public ostensibly to improve my stage presence, the truth was I did it mostly for enjoyment, my own at least, if not always the audience's. I had no illusions about a career in music.

Dana and I would play at bars and coffeehouses here and there, doing covers of R.E.M., XTC, and any other band with three initials. Dana is a great musician, so I always felt comfortable performing with him, because I knew he'd be able to cover any mistakes that I made.

Since Dana's day job was as a doorman at Catch A Rising Star, we'd sometimes practice our music on the stage in the middle of the afternoon before the club was officially open.

"Catch," as the cool people called it (and I called it that as well), had a loudspeaker mounted up on the sidewalk, so that people walking through Harvard Square could hear the bands performing in the club at night. One afternoon, we were getting really stupid, and I was throwing the word "fuck" into every line of every song I was singing. Suddenly, our friend Todd burst into the club.

"I thought that was you guys."

"How did you know we were here?"

"Because I heard you outside!"

Unbeknownst to us, we'd accidentally activated the sidewalk speaker, and thus everyone walking through the square was treated to gems such as "Fucking losing my fucking religion," and "Fucking take a fucking break fucking Driver fucking eight." The great part is, we had been doing that for at least an hour. I'll bet any parents bringing their kids to look at Harvard that weekend went away very impressed.

During another afternoon session at Catch, I noticed that somebody had come in and was watching us from a distance. We finished a song; then Dana had to go back into the office to get ready for work. The guy who'd been watching from afar approached me and said, "Hey, you guys sound great. You're really talented."

"Wow, thanks very much," I gushed. Then Dana emerged from the office, saw the guy, and said, "Excuse me sir, didn't we tell you last night you're not allowed in here anymore?" The man nodded solemnly and walked out. Dana informed me that our "fan" was actually some crazy vagrant that they had kicked out for bothering people in the restrooms.

Yet another classic example of the continual ego in-
flation followed by ego deflation that would become an
integral part of my life as an entertainer. Though not a
healthy situation, it's certainly a common one for many
in show business. And at the time, it fit right in with
what I now call my "arrogant insecurity," a roller-coaster
ride between feeling either better than, or less than, any
given person. Never did I feel equal. That's a straight
road to acute isolation.

As part of my attempt at career diversification, I taught
a course in stand-up comedy at the Boston Center for
Adult Education, which I realize sounds vaguely like a
porno establishment. Teaching someone to be funny was
sort of like teaching someone to be good looking. There
are tricks and techniques that can be learned, but without a certain natural gift, one can only achieve so much.
Since the odds of becoming a full-time comic are stacked
against most people, I tried to stress the advantages of
being humorous in any public speaking situation, so that
people could learn to make more interesting presenta-
tions at work, no matter what their job was.

As you can imagine, this type of class attracts quite an
eclectic group of people. There were genuinely funny
people who eventually did become comics; there were
accomplished writers trying to learn how to present
their material verbally; there were witty housewives who
just wanted to have fun; there were gregarious sales-
people looking to sharpen their closing skills. And, of

course, there were always a few people who thought themselves hilarious but didn't have a funny bone in their bodies. They were always the most difficult students, because when someone thinks everything they do is great, there is no room for learning anything. I remember the very first class I had, a guy came in about a half hour early and proceeded to walk around the classroom picking up items and making unfunny remarks about them, like Rip Taylor without the wit. I guess he interpreted my expression of total disgust as an invitation to continue, and he plowed ahead, finally picking up two pieces of chalk and jamming them into his nostrils. He looked at me expectantly. I stared at him for a moment, then said, "If you're looking for the real estate class, it's next door." He sulked throughout the entire first session, then afterward got a refund and never came back.

The "final exam" for the class was to perform their own material at a local comedy club. The clubs were happy to set aside an evening for my class to perform, because each student inevitably brought a slew of friends along for support, who were forced to pay full price for admission and drinks. Contrary to some accusations, I didn't see a penny of that action.

One of the first lessons I taught my students was to never blame the audience. I pontificated that even though sometimes it might actually be the crowd's fault, it was never helpful or professional to blame the people for which you were performing.

Naturally, at the "final exam" show of my very first class, I did a set before my students went on, and I struggled with the difficult audience. I was in a bad mood that evening to begin with, and when the crowd was unresponsive, I got frustrated and started berating them. As my stunned students surrounded me when I came off stage, the best I could do was mutter an embarrassed, "Hey, do as I say, not as I do!"

In a plotline right out of a B movie, I became involved with one of my students. (No, not the chalk-in-the-nose guy.) Her name was Sally, and she was a beautiful, sensitive woman who worked for a local television station. It was one of those affairs that just got hot and heavy right away, and though I had a vague sense that it was none too smart, my libido informed my brain that it was calling the shots.

Sally and I both had a large cache of neuroses. Together, we had more "issues" than your local newsstand, which made us a great fit. We weren't exactly Bogie and Bacall. More like Sid and Nancy.

I knew there would come a time in our relationship, as there had in every one of my "relationships" since college, where I'd be asked "that" question: "Do you always drink this much?" It was always asked, sometimes sooner, sometimes later, sometimes not exactly in those words, but it was always asked. I guess, privately, I knew my drinking was getting worse, because the question was coming a lot earlier in my relationships than it used to. I used to be able to date someone for months before it popped up. But in the last few years it seemed to take no more than two weeks or so into the liaison.

I always had a variety of answers at the ready, being that this question didn't catch me off guard anymore. Things such as "No, not really. I guess I've just been unwinding lately," or "I guess I've been under a little more pressure than usual lately," or sometimes the lame offering "Oh, is it the booze? I thought I was so intoxicated by you."

"Do you always drink this much?" The only honest answer was always lurking in the back of my mind: "Hell, no. I drink even more when you're not around!"

One night about a week into my affair with Sally, I was mixing drinks in my kitchen while she waited in the living room. I made her favorite drink, Coke with a splash of rum, and I made my favorite drink, rum with a splash of Coke. As soon as I carried the drinks into the living room, she said, "Wow, how much liquor did you put in those? I can smell it from here." Without missing a beat, I said, "Oh, you just smell it because I spilled some." I'd spilled it, all right. Into my glass, and down my throat.

Eventually, Sally got tired of my act, at least the one offstage. She challenged me to stop drinking. I declined to accept the challenge, because I didn't see the need for such extreme action. Oh sure, I'd dented my car a few times, and maybe I didn't work quite as hard on writing material as I should've, and maybe I had told off some important industry people when my tongue had been loosened by liquor, and maybe I occasionally forgot to do things like mail the rent check because I was off on a weekend bender. But I considered myself a functioning alcoholic, mostly because I was never drunk onstage. This kept me in denial for quite some time. Never mind the fact that the second I was offstage I immediately started drinking. Never mind the fact that when I didn't have a show at night, I drank all afternoon. As long as I didn't drink while doing my job, I was still in control.

There were certainly more than a few comics in Boston with well-earned reputations as partyers, and it seemed I never had to look very hard to find someone to compare myself with and say, "Hey, I'm not as bad as him (or her)." But as more and more of these people found recovery, there were fewer and fewer of them I could point to. That started making me nervous. I regarded it as a sort of college football poll for boozers. That guy is the worst drunk, he's number one; followed by him at number two; then her at three; then maybe me at four. As my reputation spread, I used to joke to friends about one man in particular who I felt was "much worse than me." I always said, "Hey, when *he* gets sober, then I will."

Then, the unthinkable happened. He got sober! Quite coincidentally, his career began to really take off. All I could think was *Oh, no, now I'm number one in the polls!* It bothered me a bit, but of course, not enough to quit drinking. No need to do something crazy like that.

I was performing at a ski resort in New Hampshire one weekend, and after much cajoling from Sally, I promised her that I wouldn't drink that entire weekend.

A little warning to all you folks out there. If you routinely plan when you'll drink and when you won't, chances are pretty good you're headed for trouble. "Normal," purely social drinkers don't feel the need to schedule their alcohol.

I kept my promise of not drinking, but it was sheer hell. Both nights after my shows, I paced my hotel room, unable to sleep. My heart was pounding. I felt the walls closing in on me. I was starting to get a glimpse of just how much jeopardy I was really in. My mind was racing with thought: *How did I get like this? Why is it so hard to not drink for just one night? Why do I have to live like this?*

Somehow, I made it through both nights without imbibing and drove back to Boston on Sunday morning. I couldn't wait to look Sally in the eye and tell her I'd kept my promise.

On the way to her place, I suddenly decided to celebrate my weekend of sobriety by stopping off to have a few cocktails. Time sort of got away from me, and when I called Sally from a bar to tell her how I hadn't drank all weekend, it somehow didn't impress her as much as I had hoped.

Sally ended things between us right then and there, over the phone, and I couldn't really blame her. I wished her well and went back to my seat at the bar. Oh well, there went another one. I rationalized that it was probably for the best; she would only get in the way of my career. And I certainly didn't want *anything* getting in the way of my career, I mused, as I downed yet another Scotch.

Several days later, I sat in my apartment attempting to smooth out my stand-up routine. For some reason, I didn't seem to be doing as well onstage as I used to, and I hadn't been coming up with as much new material lately, either. As I sat looking at my blank computer screen, I got very frustrated, so I figured I'd relax with a couple beers. After all, I wasn't scheduled to work that evening, so what did it matter? I kicked back with a beer or two or five or ten. I was typing things into my computer, but oddly, they didn't read as funny on the screen as they sounded in my head.

Several hours later, my phone rang, and I let the machine pick it up. I was just sober enough to realize how drunk I was, and there was no way I was in any condition to talk to anyone.

I turned up the volume and listened as my apartment was filled with the voice of a local talent agent. He was calling because some very influential network television executives were in town for the evening and wanted to scout several performers. They'd requested to see me, and the agent wanted to know if I could perform that night at a club downtown.

"Sorry for the late notice, but they just contacted me a minute ago. You're my first call. These people are only here for the day, Ed, so please call me the second you get this message, okay?" There was a loud click, and the electronic voice of my machine announced, "Tuesday, 3 p.m."

My heart sank. Why couldn't he have called me earlier? Why did it have to be tonight? He could at least have the decency to warn me! This was a day off; didn't he know I'd be "relaxing"? I knew there was no way I could sober up enough to perform that night.

I played the message over and over, torturing myself. *"Tuesday, 3 p.m., Tuesday, 3 p.m. . . ."*

They seemed like the most mocking, cruel words possible. I felt my world caving in on me. Here I'd worked so hard, almost obsessively, to have just this kind of opportunity. And now that it had finally arrived, I was too impaired to seize the moment.

"Tuesday, 3 p.m., Tuesday, 3 p.m. . . ."

I couldn't even call the agent back, and I suspected he'd figure out why I hadn't. After all, my drinking was hardly a secret. All my peers knew, and many considered me an underachiever, largely due to this very problem. I considered myself an underachiever as well, feeling that for my talent, I should be doing a lot more in the industry. But I attributed it to bad luck, a lack of the lucky breaks that I so richly deserved.

Alcoholism, which is a progressive illness, certainly threw gasoline on the fire of career frustration. Disappointment and self-pity were my daily companions. Why wasn't I receiving bigger offers? Why wasn't I famous by now? After all, hadn't I proven myself time and time again on stages, in print, on television? Why couldn't I move forward and attain the ultimate success I felt was my destiny? Why did these scouts have to show up when I was hammered? Damn my luck!

Though I didn't realize it at the time, booze, besides being a chief obstacle to happiness, fueled one of the other most insidious obstacles to peace of mind: the sense of entitlement. I felt because I had a gift for humor that I somehow deserved to have things go exactly as I wanted them to. I naively expected fame and fortune, feeling it was my inalienable birthright. I realize now that this is a ridiculous premise. Entitlement suggests that life is fair, which of course it's not. I deserve to be successful? Well, certainly, people who are blind deserve to see, and people who are deaf deserve to hear, and people who are starving deserve to eat. When put in this perspective, my insistence on having what I think I deserve looks quite petty indeed. But it's a perspective I certainly didn't have at the time.

"Tuesday, 3 p.m., Tuesday, 3 p.m. . . ."

As the cruel voice of the machine taunted me, I began sobbing uncontrollably. I had bottomed out. I was sick and tired of alcohol crippling my ability to work on my craft. I was sick and tired of embarrassing myself in front of friends and co-workers. I was sick and tired of it wreaking havoc in all areas of my life. Ultimately, I was just sick and tired of feeling sick and tired. I felt utterly defeated, physically, mentally, and spiritually. For so long I had thought that booze was my best friend, and instead it had turned out to be my worst enemy. The cumulative effect of all the drunken incidents, both big and small, had taken too big a toll. My entire life was becoming unmanageable. Terrified, I finally had to face the fact that either things would have to change, or I would eventually die from this addiction.

Once again, I found myself asking the question, "Why

do I have to live like this?'" Thank God, the answer turned out to be, I didn't have to. I made some phone calls to several of my peers and friends who had quit drinking. I had seen their lives and careers get progressively better, yet until this moment, I had dismissed any connection between their sobriety and their improved lives as merely a coincidence. Though deep inside I knew the truth, I had found it necessary to rationalize it away, in order to avoid facing the frightening reality that I would have to stop drinking in order to obtain a better life.

I got involved in a Twelve Step program. That was over a decade ago, and remains to be, by far, the best thing I've ever done. I'm still involved in this program to this day, one day at a time.

As I learned about prayer and meditation, I was able to eventually reconnect with my faith in God, a faith that had been pushed onto the back burner when I launched my career. Though I had never given up on Him, as my drinking spiraled out of control, I felt that He had perhaps given up on me. But in recovery I began to realize that He hadn't abandoned me at all.

Early on in my recuperation, I had many days where I felt like nothing but a giant, exposed nerve. Everything irritated me, and I was uncomfortable with this new concept of living life on life's terms, without the oblivion of the bottle to hide in. One particularly squirrelly afternoon, I called the man who was my sponsor in the program and complained, "If this is what sobriety feels like, I don't think I want to be sober." He then gave me what I consider to be one of the most important pieces of advice I've ever heard: "This is not what it feels like to be sober, Ed. This is what it feels like *getting* sober."

He assured me that if I toughed it out, I'd have many days ahead that were not only comfortable, but extremely happy. I told him I didn't really believe him, but that I'd give it a chance. I figured if he turned out to be wrong, I would at least have the satisfaction of saying "I told you so!" But, damn him, he turned out to be right!

Unfortunately, my newfound sobriety didn't help with my well-established unwillingness and inability to form a lasting relationship. Sally and I started dating again briefly, wanting to see how we connected when I was clear-headed. Unfortunately, this clarity merely made us see that we were not a good fit, and there were too many ghosts of our past floating around. Plus, it seemed like she wasn't interested in us as much without all the drama swirling about. We broke up for good, though for once, it was on friendly terms. While it's an old cliché, the truth was my life was really just beginning, though I wasn't sure at first if that was good news or bad news. But as I began to get involved in a Twelve Step program, and as I studied different religions and philosophies that have brought serenity and a sense of purpose to millions, several common denominators seemed to emerge, chief among them, gratitude.

I'm as guilty as anyone of taking things that I have for granted. As with so many of us, I always want more, which is not necessarily the road to happiness. So, a method many people use to keep things in perspective is a "gratitude list." It helps guard against feeling angry or anxious, at least sometimes. It's simply a list of all that one is grateful for, like friends, family, *Sports Illustrated*. Of course, if one were to actually *thoroughly* list one's blessings, starting with such basics as the ability to breathe, see, and hear, the list would be too big to ever complete. That is, of course, the very point. There's a lot to be thankful for.

Sobriety showed me that life needn't be merely a period spent staving off inevitable death. There really was a life worth living out there. And probably the most important realization I ever achieved was that no matter what had happened in the past, or what would happen in the future, I was lucky just to be alive and healthy, with food on my table and a roof over my head. I truly had all the necessities for a happy life. Anything good beyond those necessities that came to me from then on would be nothing but gravy.

Chapter

⁂5⁂

A Blind Date with Emmy

Though I had settled in somewhat comfortably, my house felt lonely. Incredibly, despite my still fresh wounds from Rita and my general mistrust of the whole dating process, I actually started thinking about climbing back up on the relationship horse. After many years of a peripatetic lifestyle, I'd finally recognized the strange but true paradox that the bigger the city, the harder it is to meet people. Although I did discover one surefire way of meeting the best-looking woman in your apartment complex: Just straggle down to your mailbox looking like you've just walked off the set of *Survivor*, and I guarantee you she'll be there. Of course, she's not around when you come home in a tuxedo carrying an Emmy, but she'll always walk by when you're standing out on the sidewalk cleaning dog crap off your shoe with a stick.

I checked out a video dating service called "Great Expectations." It seemed ridiculously expensive. Maybe I could find a cheaper one called "Very Little Hope." I also checked out a service that set up informal first meetings called "It's Just Lunch." Again, too expensive. I figured I'd wait until they open up "It's Just Pathetic." Finally, I realized that there was really only one sure way to meet "the right one," as God intended: the Internet.

It seemed like a simple revelation, really. Who among us hasn't heard about a happy couple who met online? Granted, they usually met in some sort of "Desperation Chat Room," but who am I to judge? Just point your browser to "Probingnewdepthsofdespair.com."

I decided that I would peruse the "personals" section of Yahoo! I figured Yahoo! is a good sound to associate with dating, rather than the usual, "Wow, that was quick." I made the mistake of mentioning to a writer friend of mine that I was doing this, and he immediately began forwarding, every day, via email, the most psychotic personals listings he could find. I *assume* he was doing this as a joke, but maybe he really thought I could get something special going with "Woman seeks man interested in anal sex, both giving and receiving."

I logged on to AOL and, as usual, was immediately barraged by advertising offers. This time it was, "Do you want to run Windows programs on your Mac?" Hey, I can barely run Mac programs on my Mac. I clicked on the

"No thanks" box, only because there was no box reading "Stop harassing me to buy overpriced garbage I don't want or need."

It was nice to discover that I could place a personal ad at no cost, other than my own self-respect and dignity. The site instructs people to "title" their ad, so I called mine "Facing Grim Reality." I figured I would be as up-front as possible. After all, there's nothing the ladies dig more than a deeply hurt individual whose outlook on dating has been soured by his previous relationship. I wrote out my ad, which read

> Hello, I'm a 39-year-old man with a successful career in the entertainment industry. I'm funny, honest, nice looking, and have a pretty amazing life. Yet here I am, perusing the Internet, looking for strangers. I love music (R.E.M., Springsteen, Beatles), watching sports (especially Ohio State football) and documentaries on my home theater system. I also love chess. (Now you're thinking, "Oh, *that's* why this guy is alone.") A decent man with a lot to offer looking for a decent woman with the same. I know, I know, I probably have a better chance of winning the California lottery without a ticket than meeting the right person this way, but . . . I'll give it a shot. Interested?

Wisely, people on the site use pseudonyms, and I chose to go by the name of my favorite R.E.M. song, which, appropriately enough, was "It's The End Of The

World As We Know It." I posted the ad and figured, let's see what happens. Certainly, responses would begin flooding in at any moment.

After a month of receiving no replies except from my writer friend, who by now was filling my mailbox with "men seeking men" postings on a daily basis, I finally got a hit. It came from "So Feverish," which immediately made me think she probably has herpes. The text of it follows, with my jaded reactions in italics.

Hello,

Okay, your "ad" attracted my attention and since you're likely to get plenty of responses I'll tell you a bit about me. *A weird, sort of hostile beginning. From saying "Okay, you attracted my attention" which is oddly begrudging, to the placing of the word "ad" in quotes, suggesting it may not really qualify as an ad, I'm on the defensive already. This could be the future Mrs. Driscoll!*

I am attractive, I love to laugh, and I'm emotionally stable. *That's fine, but people who are emotionally stable don't have to go around pointing it out. I pictured her typing her email using the severed fingers of past boyfriends.* My past boyfriends would say I am cute, warm, smart, fun, and enjoy being with me because I am thoughtful and treat them well. *Yeah, past boyfriends would say that, except they can't talk because you killed them.* I usually dress casually, but sometimes I like to put on a short skirt and high heels. *I like to do that sometimes, too. At least we have something in common!* Understanding the importance of chemistry, I'd like you to send me your photo, so we don't waste each other's time. *Too late. I'm not into corresponding with weirdos. You certainly won't find any on the Internet.* Would you like to follow this path a bit and see where it takes us? *No thanks. The last time I followed a path that looked like this, I ended up with poison oak.*

Okay, maybe I'm a little overly guarded. I guess I should have mentioned that fact in my "ad." But maybe "Feverish" was right: I really was likely to get plenty of responses, because the next one arrived in my online mailbox later that same day. It was from "Lucky," and I thought, well, opposites do attract, so . . .

Hi, I am an independent, sometimes too soft-hearted person. *Hmm, this seems better. Someone I can emotionally blackmail. Finally, a level playing surface.* I enjoy thought-provoking discussions, conversations, and arguments. *I don't know about the first two, but I can guarantee the third one.* I am attractive, motivated, and certainly have a mind of her own. [sic] *Hopefully, that's just bad grammar and doesn't mean she has someone else's mind for her own. I'm picturing a brain floating in a Mason jar.* What am I looking in a man? [sic] *I don't know, proof-reading ability?* I'm looking for someone with wisdom and maturity. *And I'm realizing I've just been eliminated.*

A few days later, I received the following response from "Ohbabee":

> Yes. Interested. I'm a 5' 5½" dyslexic funny woman. *Then she won't mind if I "off her blow."* I'm a serious person, prone to sudden outbursts of laughter. *I believe they call that Tourette's.* I love classical music, jazz and . . . blah, blah blah . . . this is so weird . . . anyhoo . . . I love my life . . . *What's with all the ellipses? I think I'm getting hit on by Larry King.* I think I may be your winning ticket. *A reference back to my lottery joke. I don't like people who fling my own jokes back in my face.*

Okay, maybe I'm being a bit too selective. What's this next one say?

> Hi!!!! *Already more enthusiastic than the others. Probably a crack addict.* I bet you'd like me, after all, everybody does. I meet every problem with a smile. *Wow, I'll bet that's not irritating.* My biggest passion in life is the opera. *And my biggest passion in life is* avoiding *the opera.*

Hmm, here's one of the more interesting ones:

> I am a transsexual woman who has had my operation, so I'm 100% female. You'd never know the difference. *I'm betting I would.* I'm actually quite old-fashioned. *Yeah, a real Norman Rockwell type of transsexual.* I'm a combination of sexpot and the girl next door. *And the boy next door, too.* I'm com-

pletely nonmaterialistic. *I guess so, you didn't mind parting with that penis.*

This one came from "I Am Special."

Hello, your ad caught my eye. What can I tell you about me? I like Fridays more than Mondays. *Wow, you are special.* I'm 31, but look 21. I get carded at the liquor store all the time! *You're at the liquor store all the time? Now there's a selling point.* Dancing is my biggest hobby, along with tennis and becoming a doctor. *Now that's what you want in a doctor, someone who considers medical care to be a "hobby."* I'm a creature of habit with a rebellious nature. I'm unpredictable, but that's part of my immense charm. Can you see where this is going? *Yes, I can. It's called a "wastebasket."*

This one appeared in my emailbox, from "SusieQ."

Hi. I decided to respond to your ad, though I normally am only interested in people in the 30–36 range. *Well, I'm truly honored.* I am certainly a genuine and real person with zero attitude. Would you like to meet for dinner? *Yeah, why don't you come over between 5 and 7? That's when they feed us at the old folks home.*

So, who's next?

Hello. I am a tall Dutch girl. *At least I know she'll pay for her own dinner.* I love the ocean. There's no such thing as a bad beach! *Yeah? Ever see* Saving

Private Ryan? I have thick long legs, nice teeth, nice eyes, nice feet, and good character. *I don't know whether I should date her, or run her in the Kentucky Derby... It's "Mrs." Ed!*

I got this one from "Heart Smart," which I believe is a butter substitute:

I am a normal girl, and live in LA. *Well, which is it?* I love French gardens, colorful perennials, fragrant soaps, sailboats on the ocean, floating candles, and rainbow-colored beach umbrellas. *When the acid trip's over, look me up.*

I got this response from "Confident One."

I am 46, but don't resemble my age. I like to dress wild. I'm a part-time cosmologist. I'm very curvy, with maybe a few extra pounds. I have four children, but they are all grown. Sorry I don't have a picture for you. *That's okay, I think I've got one in my head.* I enjoy walks around the block. *What is she, a beagle?* I believe a man should fall in love with me as a person, and sex is just a bonus. *A bonus? Great, once a year, at Christmas time.* I guess I'm a bit conceited, but what can I say? I am a very rare find. *Well, so's a case of polio.*

I got this one from "Cal-Gal."

Hello, I found your ad interesting. I'm a 40-year-old, divorced woman in her third year of sobriety, with no baggage. *Except for that huge carry-on marked "Utter Denial."*

As they say at football games, "after further review," I decided that the Internet was better left to be used by others for its original purposes: passing highly classified military secrets and downloading pictures of Anna Kournikova. Hell, I've got a lot of work to do on my new house and a busy career, I told myself. A relationship, or even attempting to have one, is hopeless. I'm giving up on it all forever, for good, that's it. This time, it's definite . . . for today, anyway.

≷ ≷

It was pretty shocking how quickly the career gravy began flowing once I quit drinking. I had exactly one week to move from Boston to LA in 1994. I had opened for Dennis Miller at some colleges in New York, and he'd hired me to write on his new show *Dennis Miller Live* on HBO. I loaded up my belongings in my Ford Escort and drove across the country. Production was beginning almost immediately, and I didn't even have time to look for an apartment. Fortunately, a friend in LA told me of an opening in his building and I was able to sign a lease by fax as I made my way west. The lease was for a year, which was a bit scary considering that Dennis's show only had a commitment of six episodes at that point. However, I agreed to the twelve-month term, rolling with my newfound optimism that things would work out for me as long as I stayed aboard the "gravy" train.

I realized that this job was probably the "big break" I had been looking for since I first took the stage back in eighth grade, and consequently it was hard to sleep the night before my first day at the show. I was due at the office at CBS Television City at 8 a.m., and my mind was in overdrive as I anticipated what it would all be like. In an incredibly brilliant move, I somehow forgot to reset my alarm clock from Eastern time to Pacific time and didn't realize that I was up and showering at 3 a.m. instead of 6 a.m. I thought it looked a bit dark outside, but figured this was that "morning marine layer" the locals talked about.

As I was driving in, I saw that my dashboard clock read four in the morning, and I realized what I'd done. I didn't know what else to do but show up at the studio. It's good to be eager, but this looked pretty silly. The guard at the gate was literally sleeping when I arrived.

I was too embarrassed to tell any of my new co-workers what I'd done. The worst part was that at about one in the afternoon, my lack of sleep caught up with me, and I was dragging through the rest of the day. I drank so much coffee that when I peed, a stirrer came out. An inauspicious beginning, to be sure.

I worked with a fun and talented group of people, including Jeff Cesario, Kevin Rooney, Eddie Feldmann, David Feldman, and Greg Greenberg. Dennis took phone calls on the air, and he wanted some of the writers to screen those calls in order to determine which ones would be the most entertaining. Greg and I volunteered for screener duty. We thought it might be funny to hear how strange some of the callers were, and we weren't disappointed. For every good, intelligent viewer with a question we sent through to Dennis and his guest during the show, there were ten unstable people who would have been better off calling the suicide prevention hotline. We got everything from obscene propositions to confused foreigners trying to order parts for their lawnmower.

The amazing thing was that the phone lines were completely lit up (as were many of the callers) by 6 p.m. for a show that went on the air live at 11:30 p.m. That truly amazes me still. If I wanted to wait on hold for hours to ask one question, I'd just call Farmers Insurance company.

Once during rehearsal, I made the mistake of putting through one of the people who was on hold. Dennis didn't realize it was a real caller and, thinking it was one of us, proceeded to profanely belittle him as he tried to ask a question. There was an awkward silence; then the poor caller said, "Wow, Dennis, I just wanted to ask a question. I don't think you need to be swearing at me." Dennis asked, "Isn't this one of the writers?" and when it became clear it wasn't, he said, "Well, hang on then, because I think we're going to have a job opening after this." Luckily, he turned out to be kidding.

One afternoon, we were going over the material for the show, and I was pushing hard for Dennis to do a joke I'd written. He was reluctant, yet I baited him by saying,

"Well, it's funny and intelligent, and *if delivered properly, it should get a huge laugh.*" That was clearly throwing the gauntlet at Dennis's feet, and he said, "Okay, Drisc, if you feel that strongly, let's do it."

Looking back, I see that the idea of the joke was solid, but it wasn't quite fleshed out. I was trying to make the point that in the Medicare debate, the Democrats were citing a lot of statistics, while the Republicans were really just tugging at emotions with fluff. Anyway, here's the "As Broadcast" script of that "can't miss" joke:

AS BROADCAST 8/18/95
OPENING MONOLOGUE

DENNIS

Democrats and Republicans released competing ad campaigns this week to promote their views of the Medicare debate. The Democratic commercials feature statistics showing that callous cuts in Medicare will force the elderly to pay more than they can afford, while the Republican ads feature the Statue of Liberty, Mt. Rushmore, and the flag.

COMPLETE SILENCE

DENNIS (CONT'D)

So, uhh . . . Where's Ed Driscoll? Hey, I told you that . . . I told you that was going to eat shit. "Oh, no, it's a smart joke, oh." Now I'm fucking crucified out here . . . and you're back there having a Snapple. I lost a couple of heat tiles on that one.

BIG LAUGH

Baskin-Robbins this week introduced Polar Pizza, a frozen confection made to resemble a pizza. Dominos immediately threatened to sue, saying *they* have exclusive rights to deliver ice-cold pizza.

BIG LAUGH

DENNIS (CONT'D)

So Ed, my young friend, you can do all the deep jokes you want. But if you want behavior mod, you go to the Domino pizza joke.

LAUGHTER

DENNIS (CONT'D)

Finally, in Oregon, seventy-year-old Hazel Helen Gessler, a great grandmother, was charged with dealing marijuana after police discovered fourteen bags of pot in her home. Mrs. Gessler's family told police that the fact she always has pot is what makes her a *great* grandmother.

BIG LAUGH

This was yet another major dose of the mixture of humiliation and acclamation so endemic to a life in show business. An ego-raising, spirit-crushing cocktail that messes with your head far more than even a cocktail containing alcohol. And for me, both were equally addictive.

After all, how many people have the chance to be publicly scolded for their work on national TV? Fortunately, it was done in a spirit of fun, and when I apologized about the joke afterward, Dennis said he was actually glad about the way it had gone. He'd turned it into a fun moment, and the audience enjoyed it. Still, I figured it was probably a good thing for me that I had written the pizza and the grandmother jokes as well.

Dennis's show did two tremendous things for me. It enabled me to win an Emmy award, and it introduced me to Rita. Okay, the show did *one* tremendous thing for me. I just thought it was two at the time.

When it was first announced that I, along with my coworkers, had been nominated for the Emmy in the category of "outstanding writing," I was completely dazed. How had I gone from being rejected by a small-time greeting card manufacturer to being touted for the ultimate prize in television? It just didn't seem possible.

I realized that I would have to brace myself to be okay, whether I won or lost. Losing was a higher probability, of course. After all, actress Susan Lucci had been nominated nineteen times and had won only once.

The night of the awards, as I sat in the auditorium

and listened to Jerry Seinfeld read the names of the various nominees, I bowed my head and asked God to give me the strength to deal with whatever happened. Instantly, I felt at peace and was truly braced to hear someone else win. But suddenly Jerry said, "The Emmy goes to . . ." followed by our names. It was totally surreal. At first I thought I'd just imagined it. But as my fellow scribes jumped to their feet, I finally realized that it was actually happening.

On my way to the stage, I stopped to pump Jay Leno's hand as I passed him in the aisle. I was in such a dreamlike state that I didn't even remember doing so until I watched the moment on television later. I was a bit embarrassed when the replay showed that Jay was nice enough to offer his hand, and I was so excited I looked as though I was going to jump into his lap. You can actually see the relief on Jay's face as I continued past him down the aisle.

I floated up onto the stage and stood clutching my trophy as Dennis spoke on our behalf. I'm sure his speech was great, but I didn't hear any of it. I was too preoccupied with surveying the auditorium and soaking it all in, like a biscuit in gravy, appropriately enough.

As I stood backstage in a daze, I suddenly found myself face-to-face with Barbra Streisand. She looked at me, pointed at the statue and asked, "Is that yours?" I opened my mouth to say something, anything, but for the first time in my life, nothing came out. She smiled and walked away. I'm still not sure if she was being friendly or was genuinely suspicious that I had sneaked behind the curtain and was attempting to abscond with somebody's Emmy. It was all so incredible, it sort of felt like I actually was stealing one.

As the press took photos and interviewed us, it finally began to sink in, and I started to enjoy myself.

At one point in the evening, actress Tori Spelling approached and asked if she could touch my Emmy. I resisted the urge to say, "Go ahead, it's as close as you'll ever get." Hey, how about that? My first award, and I was already thinking like a Hollywood prick.

The greatest part of it all was the teary phone call I got to make to my parents back in Pittsburgh. It seemed that finally, all the heartache and struggle and sweat and toil had paid off handsomely, and I was thrilled because they were thrilled. Even though they didn't always understand why I had to be in this business—I'm not sure I totally understood either—they were always incredibly supportive, probably more so than I would have been in their situation.

When I got home that night, I couldn't believe how many phone messages I had. There was a barrage at six o'clock Pacific, because the awards were being aired live on the East Coast, then another barrage of calls at nine o'clock Pacific when the West Coast saw the tape delay. I hate to sound so corny, but it was truly incredible to hear family and friends crying with joy into my answering machine. I've never been so moved. To this day, I've saved all the messages.

I had to laugh, in the middle of all the emotional calls, my friend Jim had checked in to discuss a possible trade in our fantasy football league. He'd completely forgotten that the Emmys were going on and just happened to call when everyone else did. It was a healthy reminder to me that not everybody in the world is wrapped up in what happens in show business.

I was totally appreciative of how fortunate I was: a career taking off, a personal life filled with caring friends and family who shared in my triumphs. The gravy was overflowing.

A few days later, I flew back to Pittsburgh and surprised my parents and sisters by bringing the Emmy with me. It was fun seeing the reactions of the X-ray security people at the different airports. They didn't bat an eye in LA, and one guy said to me, "We sure have seen a lot of these going through the last few days." Wow, it was a good thing I wasn't traveling by boat, because he sure took the wind out of my sails. But in Pittsburgh and Columbus, security people were definitely interested in it, and they all made me take it out of the bag and display it. I convinced several of them it was actually a bowling trophy.

The best part of it all was to sit back and watch friends fawn over the statue. The pride in their eyes made me happy. It was also the weekend of the long-awaited Ohio State–Notre Dame showdown, and on a beautiful sunny day, I got to see my beloved Bucks lay it on the Irish. For me, life just didn't get any sweeter than that.

Or so I thought. But amazingly, life got much sweeter. When I got back from Columbus, I finally found the gumption to call and ask Rita out. She readily agreed, then said something interesting.

"Ed, I'm really glad you called, but I have to say, it sure took you long enough. I'm actually pretty surprised to hear from you."

"Really? Wow, I thought you knew I had a crush on you."

"Oh, I did know, but I just didn't think you were ever going to act on it."

"Why's that?"

"Well, do you remember how you were always inviting me to come up and visit you at the Dennis Miller offices?"

"Sure."

"Do you remember that one day when I finally did, and you immediately went into your office and shut the door?"

"Um, no, actually, I don't. Oh, wait, yeah, I do. Yeah, I had a bunch of jokes due and I was way behind on them. But, you were talking to your friend Holly, so I assumed that's why you were there."

"You sure are a hopeless romantic, Ed."

Well, touché. And she was certainly right about it taking a long time. It was months earlier that I had first bumped into Rita, quite literally.

I was in the CBS commissary, my head distracted by ideas I was mulling over for Dennis's monologue, and as I absentmindedly reached for a tray, I bumped into a woman and knocked her soup right onto the floor. This certainly brought me back to earth from wherever I was, and I instinctively dropped to my knee and started trying to save what soup I could, as if someone would want to eat it at that point. I looked up to see who my unintended victim was, and immediately stared into the prettiest eyes I'd ever seen.

She introduced herself as Rita, a producer at CBS, and I introduced myself as Ed, a klutz at HBO. She invited me to join her for lunch, pointing out that the soup already was on me.

We ran into each other, figuratively, quite a few times over the next several weeks. A big part of me desperately wanted to ask her out, yet my old, established fears of complicating my life with a possible relationship kept me ambivalent about it all.

But following my return to LA from back east, I made the aforementioned phone call, and Rita and I started seeing each other constantly, and fell madly in love.

It was a relationship like I'd never experienced before. For whatever reason, everything between us just felt so effortless. It all made sense to me now. My career was in high gear, and my personal life was finally catching up. After just a few months, I once again found myself down on my knee in front of Rita, only this time it wasn't to clean up soup, but to propose.

For so long, I had thought I could never get married. But clearly I hadn't been ready for such a commitment. I had to quit drinking to get to this point. It was time to settle down. Everything was perfect. I was practically drowning in gravy.

≋ ≋

As days went by after my negative Internet dating experiment, I started feeling open to dating again. Under the pretense of attending a game at Dodger Stadium together, a bunch of my friends ganged up on me in a sort of "relationship intervention." They tried to convince me to date some of the "top choice candidates" they (most likely, their wives or girlfriends) had lined up for me. They must have felt there wasn't quite enough misery in my life. They insisted on setting me up, and believe me, there's a reason it's called "setting someone up."

I whined about how troubled my relationships had been in the past, and of course, being good friends, they naturally blamed me. "You have to stop dating flaky chicks," said one. It sounded to me like a breakfast cereal. "Enjoy a nice big bowl of sugar-frosted flaky chicks."

As the Dodgers' pitchers got hammered, my friends continued to hammer at me, telling me about all the "nice girls" they were sure I'd want to meet. Finally, and with more than a small amount of trepidation, I agreed to let them set up a few blind dates for me.

I dated Debbie for a couple of weeks, and it was surprisingly pleasant. She seemed very mellow, and we enjoyed many nice conversations over dinner. It seemed too good to be true.

One afternoon, I received a call from her. She sounded a bit strained as we made small talk, and I thought she was just having a bad day. It turns out she was having a bad millennium. After I asked her if she wanted to go to dinner that night, she blurted out, "Do you have a problem opening the car door for me?" I thought for a moment, then replied, "I don't think so. Because if I recall correctly, I do open the car door for you." "Not all the time," she shot back, citing a specific evening when we were getting into my car to drive her home. I thought back to that night, recalling that my hands were full because I was carrying a bunch of her stuff to load into the trunk and . . . wait a minute. I have to defend myself over this now? This woman clearly required more maintenance than the Space Shuttle.

Of course, I handled her criticism with maturity. "Maybe you should date a valet," I said evenly. Then, she delivered the real punch line: "My ex-husband used to leave me standing out in the rain, so I'm not letting you get away with it."

Okay, I could definitely hear the strains of the theme from *Psycho* at this point. Sorry, but I'm like the airlines. I only allow one carry-on. The rest of the baggage has to be checked. "I'm sorry that he treated you that way," I said, "but I don't think it's fair for you to take it out on me, do you?"

"You guys are all the same," she snapped.

Uh-oh. Now my spider sense was definitely tingling. I hadn't seen a red flag this big since the end of the Soviet Union. I politely suggested that perhaps we shouldn't see each other again, which, incredibly, seemed to shock her. Debbie said, "I'm just being honest with you." I appreciate honesty, but if a woman told me, "May I be honest with you? I'd like to attack you with a machete," I'd appreciate *that* honesty, but I wouldn't want to date her, either.

The next woman I went out with, Melinda, lived quite a distance away from me, which would eventually turn out to be a blessing for both of us. She offered to pick me up for our date, which I thought was a nice gesture. Also, it would give me a chance to harangue her if she didn't open the car door for me, thus striking a blow for men's equality.

She pulled up to my house right on time, and as we weaved our way through Hollywood, she certainly had a lot to say. Unfortunately, none of it was directed to me. Melinda's cell phone had rang right as she'd picked me up, and she'd instantly become deeply involved in a conversation with her friend Suzie. It's not like she ignored me completely, though. Every few minutes she'd assure me that she'd be "finished in a second. You don't mind, do you?"

Hey, why would I mind? She hadn't talked to Suzie even once in the hour since they'd last seen each other. Far be it from me to come between two long lost friends.

Melinda was just the type of driver that drove me crazy. Before I knew her, when I saw a car swerving in and out of lanes, I assumed the driver was drunk. Now I just assume they're yakking on a cell phone. Often, it turns out to be a drunk on a cell phone. And it's always an important conversation, something like, ";Hi, it's Marge, just wanted to let you know I'll be a little late because I'm about to cause a sixty-two-car pileup on the interstate." Hands-free phones seem like a nice solution, but it still won't protect us from the brains-free people using them. If you're going to talk on the phone as your car careens about like Gary Busey at nickel beer night, why don't you just load up your trunk with explosives and get it over with?

About halfway to the movie theater, we nearly plowed into a street vendor after running a light that was as red as my face, with the oblivious Melinda chatting happily away on her phone. I decided I'd had enough of driving with Popeye Doyle, and after several unsuccessful attempts to get her attention, I finally pulled out my cell phone and called her. Melinda clicked over with her call waiting, and I said, "Hi, it's your date. I'm calling from the passenger seat, and I'd like to not have to call you from the emergency room, so can you hang up with Suzie now?"

We arrived at the theater early, because when you're driving that fast, you tend to make good time. After a quick check to make sure there were no pedestrians impaled on the grill of her car, we went in to see the movie.

Of course, as is the norm now, they showed seventy-five previews before the main attraction began. It's reached the point where by the time they start showing the movie I actually came to see, I'm sick of watching movies. At last, the "featured attraction" flickered across the screen, but right at that moment Melinda turned to me and began talking in the same loud voice she'd used on her phone. Wow, this woman was certainly touching all the bases. It was as though she were working off some sort of "Ed's pet peeves" checklist.

As she yakked in my ear, I tried to "shhh" her, which only caused her to talk louder in order to be heard above my "shhh"-ing. I would have been embarrassed, except that as usual, the theater was filled with nothing but other ill-mannered rubes conversing at high volume during the film.

It never ceases to amaze me how loudly, and how often, people talk during films these days. When I was a kid, people got kicked out for coughing. Now, it's like Mardi Gras in there, but less inhibited. I suppose there are many reasons for this horrifying trend, such as the elimination of ushers. Also, because of VCRs and DVD players, people watch movies at home and talk to each other throughout the film, and many aren't bright enough to realize that carrying this behavior over into a theater where others are trying to watch the movie is incredibly inconsiderate and inappropriate. It's not a matter of a few folks whispering occasionally. Most movies I attend at public theaters nowadays sound like the floor of the stock exchange.

Needless to say, when Melinda dropped me off later that night, we both knew it was the last we'd be seeing of each other. But I didn't regret going out with her, because she inspired in me a tremendous business idea.

It's now my goal to open a series of movie houses where no talking *whatsoever* is tolerated. I don't care if you're having a heart attack, you can drag yourself out to the lobby and *quietly* call for an ambulance. Anyone who did talk would be immediately treated to a twenty thousand–volt burst of electricity sent through their seat. Their next of kin could then claim their ashes *quietly* once the film had ended.

The dating hit parade just kept on coming. Next up was Brenda, a woman whose voice sounded like Fran Drescher's, only more grating. She constantly sang along to my car radio. The fact that I listen to talk radio made it especially annoying. The big payoff came when I was giving her a tour of my home. As we walked to the guesthouse, where I have my office, she told me she had dated some "idiot" who actually collected different baseball caps and displayed them on his wall. As I keyed us into my office, which was completely covered with ball caps I'd been collecting all my life, the best I could manage was a sickly "Well, I'll bet his hats weren't as cool as any of these." She was unimpressed, as was I. It turned out we did have one thing in common, though. We both agreed we shouldn't date each other. With apologies to Pearl Harbor, it seemed that all my dates lived in infamy.

My friends introduced me to a woman named Tiffany, and we ended up dating for several weeks. She was a spiritual person, though she had the type of spirituality that I personally found a little weird. New Age stuff, you know, a bunch of theories about how when people die, their souls become pine trees. Shit like that. But I enjoyed her company. She was pretty and very sweet, with the only real caveat being that she seemed to start getting serious almost immediately. While I found it a bit stifling, she was so sincere and honest about her feelings that I wasn't all that spooked. In truth, I think I was flattered and grateful for the attention. She talked in vaguely permanent terms when she spoke of our future.

With her flaky nature, I should have expected what happened next, but once again, I somehow was caught off guard. One afternoon, Tiffany showed up at my house in an almost frenzied state. In complete seriousness, she told me that she'd been sitting at a restaurant eating French fries when it dawned on her that it was a sign she should move to France. I told her that was quite a coincidence, because earlier I'd been eating German potato salad and realized it was a sign I should invade Poland.

She was nice enough to invite me to go with her to Paris, but I declined. I told her I prefer warmer climates and that if she ended up eating any Jamaican jerk chicken, she should give me a call.

Next up was Gretchen, who seemed like a nice person. And I suppose she might have been, but when she came over to my house, she eyed my décor and said, "Ugh. Do you have to have so much Ohio State memorabilia? Who cares about all that stupid, rah-rah stuff? It's pretty juvenile, don't you think?" No, juvenile was when

I gave her the finger behind her back as she was leaving. Mature was knowing not to call her again.

Later that evening, following this latest romantic success, I ended up having dinner at a neighborhood sports bar, attempting to explain to my well-meaning buddies why it just hadn't worked out with me and the women they'd set me up with.

I told them that maybe I was in some weird form of denial, but I preferred to put my energies into my work. After all, when work was disappointing, at least I still got paid. My friend Jim said, "On his deathbed, no man says he wishes he'd spent more time at the office." To which I replied, "Oh, yeah? What if he's a porn star?"

By the end of the evening, all my buddies seemed resigned to the fact that I was not going to hook up with any of their dating candidates anymore. Stubbornly, I had worn the boys down, as much as their "perfect for you" girls had worn me down. We all walked out of the sports bar together in awkward silence. Finally, one of my friends turned to me and blurted out, "Hey, you're not gay, are you?"

Chapter

⚡6⚡

Me and Oscar

I n 1996, everything seemed to be going my way. I reluctantly left *Dennis Miller Live* at the advice of my management who wanted me to branch out in other areas. Though I'd miss working at Dennis's show, I decided to give notice because I ultimately wanted to push myself in as many different creative directions as possible. I was determined to explore just how far my abilities could take me. I was inundated with offers for many intriguing projects, and I embraced my new challenges with vigor.

Oddly, though things were going as well as I could possibly hope for, I began to feel pangs of discontentment. I wasn't really sure why. I ignored the feelings, figuring they were the natural by-product of the restlessness that all humans feel from time to time. I was busy performing and was writing for other comedians as well, such as Howie Mandell and Louie Anderson.

Louie is a terrific comic and a terrific person. I first met him when he was looking for someone to help him put together a set for the *Tonight Show,* and Jeff Cesario recommended me. The first time I showed up at Louie's apartment, we engaged in some small talk; then I started up my computer and said, "Well, let's get to it, shall we?" Louie rolled his eyes and said in mock-disgust, "Oh no, you're one of these jerks who actually wants to work, huh?" I said, "Hey, I don't care; you're the one who's gonna be up there doing this crap." Thus began our working relationship.

I started hanging out with Louie, and he taught me a lot about how a celebrity should conduct himself. He's highly recognizable, of course, and like Henny Youngman, he really has a knack for making people not only laugh, but feel good about themselves. I was impressed by the happy, grateful faces of people he complimented as we browsed through their stores, or folks he stopped to talk with on the street. He emphasized to me that no matter how big one became in show business, one must always have time for people. He told me that a true "star" is one that treats everyone equally well. His philosophy was to "share the gravy." He made me promise that when I really hit it "big," I'd still be the same nice person. I jokingly asked him, "And if my career goes downhill, can I start treating people like shit?" Louie said, "Actually, if your career goes bad, I'd advise you to treat people even nicer!"

At the time, I didn't know Louie's manager, Ahmos Hassan. But in another example of Louie's generosity, he asked Ahmos to come watch me at a club in LA one night. To avoid feeling extra nervous before my show, I tried to fool myself by dismissing Ahmos's appearance at the club as no big deal. However, there was no getting past the fact that if he took an interest in me, it would be a highly significant step up for my career.

I decided I'd open that night with a joke about representation, just to make things more interesting for Ahmos. I took the stage and said, "My career is going great. That's because I have a rich and powerful agency backing me. They're called the Unemployment Bureau." It got a big laugh, and it set the tone for a good show.

Afterward, Ahmos approached me and we went out for coffee. I was struck by his almost ethereal approach to a business that regularly brings out the worst in people. He was honest, which I respected, and he was extremely impressed with me, which, of course, I respected even more! When our conversation turned to a mutual love of Big Ten football, I realized that here was a guy who could be far more than a manager to me. He was someone who could be a close and trusted friend. That's exactly what he turned into, despite the disturbing fact that he had attended OSU's bitter archrival the University of Michigan. The only time of the year we don't talk about football is the week of the Ohio State–UM showdown.

I signed with Ahmos that very evening, and he told me his first task as my new manager would be to get me a big-time agent. Our reputations, his firmly established and mine growing rapidly, combined with my writing samples, allowed us access to the most powerful agencies in Hollywood.

It boggled my mind that I was being courted by these agents who also represented some of the biggest names in the industry. In the back of my mind was often the thought, *What is a kid from Pittsburgh doing here with these people? Maybe I should steal an ashtray to prove I was actually in this building.*

I ultimately signed with Richard Weitz at ICM, one of the world's premiere talent agencies. Richard was highly regarded as one of the top young agents in town, and I was pleased to be working with him. Richard later became a partner in another highly influential agency, Endeavor, and I followed him there.

Richard gave me some interesting insight regarding the dynamics of show business. Early on in our working relationship, I'd made the incredible mistake of showing up at a meeting with a studio executive ten minutes ahead of the scheduled time. In my mind, that's not really very early at all, but when Richard heard that, he told me, "Never show up early; it makes them think you're too eager!" Amazing. Only in Hollywood is being punctual interpreted as desperation. Here I was, naively thinking I was merely being polite by being on time, not realizing that by doing so I was practically wearing a sign saying, "Will work for food." In spite of how it appears, I still like to show up a little before my appointment time, even if the person I'm meeting feels compelled to make me wait in the lobby for a while out of principle. It never ceases to amaze me—I'll walk in for a noon meeting at 11:55 a.m., and the stunned receptionist will say, "Wow, you're early!"

As my agent and manager introduced me to the upper echelon of show biz, one success begat another, and I developed a reputation that allowed me to work with some of my favorite celebrities.

I got the opportunity to write some jokes for one of my favorite sportscasters, Bob Costas. I sent him lines for some banquets. It was fun working with him, even though it was all over the phone, he in St. Louis, myself in LA. Bob's accounting people were late sending my payment, and while I wasn't really concerned, he sent me a funny note thanking me for not sending any thugs after him to collect my money. We finally met face-to-face a few years later when I was a Creative Consultant on *The Drew Carey Show*, and he was a guest performer.

My friend Steve Levy, a talented and successful actor, who at the time lived in the same apartment complex as I, was always amused by the messages left by high-profile people on my answering machine. One time Steve was over when I was checking them, and he heard "Hi Ed, Bob Costas." For some reason, this tickled him, and from then on, whenever Steve would call me, whether I answered or he got the machine, he'd always open the conversation with, "Hi Ed, Bob Costas."

He did this for weeks, and I always expected it. One day, the phone rang, and when I picked it up I heard, "Hi

Ed, Bob Costas." Affecting a silly, lilting, singsong voice, I replied, "Oh, hi, Bobby. How are you there, pally? Huh? How's it going, Bob?" There was a brief pause; then I heard "Uh, I'm fine." It was the real Bob Costas, and I could tell he was as surprised as I was.

I briefly considered telling him why I had spoken to him in that bizarre voice, but quickly realized that explaining, "Oh, every time my friend calls, he says he's you," was even creepier than what I had just done. So, I simply went right into the conversation in my normal voice as if nothing had happened. I was cringing the entire time. In retrospect, I probably should have just told Bob the truth, but I had just started working with him and was too horrified to do so. There's a lesson in there somewhere, but I'm not really sure what it is.

Though collaborating with a sportscaster like Bob was certainly a change of pace from my usual work with stand-up comedians, it was far from my most unusual writing job. That honor would go to the time I was contacted by a friend of a friend of a friend about writing some material for Kato Kaelin.

Yep, that was my initial reaction as well. This was just a few months after the infamous trial, and Kato, who had actually done stand-up and a lot of acting long before he became internationally known, was looking to "punch up" his routine.

Initially I refused, because, being as misinformed about him as most other people, I believed him to be nothing but an opportunist, taking advantage of other people's horrible circumstances. But his representatives kept asking me to at least meet with him before I turned him down.

They had also contacted a friend of mine, comic/writer Jhoni Marchinko, now co-executive producer of *Will & Grace*, about working with Kato as well. She shared my reservations, but together we reluctantly agreed to meet the most famous witness since Jehovah.

The circumstances surrounding the clandestine meeting had the feel of a powwow with Deep Throat of Watergate lore. Jhoni and I were instructed to go to a vacant LA office building late at night and speak to the guards in order to be escorted upstairs. Though this secrecy seemed a bit over-the-top paranoid to me, it was at a time when Kato's every move was constantly shadowed by paparazzi.

I'm certainly not one of those people who believes that *any* publicity is good publicity. You want to be a household name? Well, Judas is one.

On my way to meet Kato, I mused about my own admittedly miniscule amount of fame. Would I ever want the type of attention that major celebrities receive? Well, I guess I was in the classic mode of wanting my cake and eating it, too. I wanted the money and perks and conveniences of being internationally famous, but without any of the hassle. I once asked my manager to check and see if that was possible. Oddly, he never got back to me on that.

So I went to the meeting with very preconceived anger toward this guy, really wanting to hate him. I was certainly taken aback when I actually spoke with Kato. I grilled him pretty intensely about his role in the whole sordid affair, and I soon learned a lot that, sadly for his sake, he and his representatives were never able to convey to the public.

For instance, he didn't just decide to become an actor when he became America's most famous houseguest. He'd been working for years at the acting trade, landing many small roles, and while his profile had obviously been raised, he found in actuality that he was getting less acting work than before, because people saw him as somehow sympathetic to Simpson. In reality, he'd not been a very good witness, but only because he was badly coached, and he never attempted to intentionally protect a guy whom he believed to be guilty.

I also learned that he'd turned down literally millions of dollars for such things as the marketing of a Kato doll, because he didn't want to crassly cash in on his new infamy. I asked him, "What does a Kato doll do? You wind it up and it crashes on your couch?"

It soon became very evident to Jhoni and me that Kato was certainly no villain, so we agreed to work with him. We wrote some material for Kato, and he performed in some clubs in LA. It was interesting to see people's reaction when he was introduced. Some were polite, some booed, and all were surprised to see him up there. He did fairly well, but eventually lost interest in comedy, much as the media lost interest in him. As far as I know, he continues to audition for acting roles and take his craft quite seriously, and also continues to be a good father to his daughter.

One of my more ridiculous performing experiences occurred around that time as well. I was slated to appear on *The Jerry Lewis Telethon,* and I was happy to be lending some time, if not actual talent, to the cause. Several other comics and I were to be taped at the Improv in Hollywood a few weeks before Labor Day; then the segments would be aired throughout the telethon.

I was a bundle of nervous energy as I waited to hear my name called by MC Norm Crosby, legendary comic best known as the master of the malaprop. Just as he introduced me, my contact lens rolled up inside my eye. If I had been thinking quick enough, I would have asked for the taping to be stopped while I fixed it. But it all happened so fast, and it was in front of a live crowd, so I just proceeded toward the stage. It was surreal, to see a blurry Norm Crosby shaking my hand and to turn into the bright lights and cameras and attempt to be funny. The pain in my eye was excruciating—or "excommunicating," as Crosby might have called it. Having one clear eye and one foggy one completely threw off my equilibrium. It was like trying to perform while standing on top of a galloping horse as someone threw sand in my eye.

I ended up doing okay, but afterward I was pretty distraught. I knew I could have done better if I had been in a normal state, and I feared what it would look like when it played on television. Logically, as I considered the plight of the unfortunate people for whom this telethon was being held, I realized that any of my little disappointments or problems were embarrassingly petty. Yet despite this obvious reality, I couldn't shake my self-absorbed concerns.

I was a basket case when I got home that night, which further exacerbated my already strained relations with Rita. After four increasingly bumpy years together, we were both pretty unsympathetic to each other's complaints by this point. What little communication we'd once had was now nonexistent, and we'd basically retreated into our own separate little worlds. Old anxieties and cynicism about the male-female dynamic filled my head.

When my segment aired on the telethon, I was shocked at how normal I actually looked. Anybody who didn't know what had happened couldn't really tell. I went from initially being disappointed to feeling that it really was one of my best performances ever, considering what was going on up there. However, this reprieve didn't really placate me. In fact, nothing did anymore. My problems with Rita had me in a state of perpetual unhappiness, despite my myriad of satisfying professional achievements.

One evening, as Rita and I were exiting the front door of the house we had purchased together, on our way to yet another counseling session, to make yet another attempt at rekindling feelings that had been gone so long we could barely remember them, she stopped cold and looked at me.

"This is over," she said, without a trace of emotion.

"What is?" I asked, as if I didn't know what she was talking about.

She looked at me sadly, shook her head, and went back inside the house. I followed her in and closed the door.

Rita sat down, accidentally plopping herself onto the TV remote control I'd left in the chair. She held it up toward me. "How many times have I asked you to not leave this here?" Somehow I guessed it was a rhetorical question, so I said nothing and sat in a chair opposite her.

For several silent minutes, Rita stared at the floor, absentmindedly rolling the remote through her fingers. Finally, she looked up and said, "This just isn't working, Ed."

"Well, maybe it needs new batteries."

"That's exactly what I'm talking about! Everything's one big joke to you, isn't it?"

"Do you see me laughing?" I snapped back.

Rita's face flushed with anger. "You have a lot of growing up to do, Ed, but I'm not going to hang around waiting for you to do it. We're finished. So, either you can leave, or you can stay and I'll leave, but one thing is for sure—we're never staying here together again."

"Fine," I said, as coolly as possible. Ignoring Rita's tears and desperately attempting to stifle my own, I stuffed some clothes into a garment bag and left. As I drove aimlessly into the chilly evening, all of the old fear, distrust, and outrage that I wasn't getting what I deserved came crashing down on me. Somehow, the gravy had disappeared, and I wasn't sure if I would ever see it again.

≳ ≲

That's how I ended up in my new house, full of old problems. What caused me to end up in this position? Was it a fact that things in my life had changed for the worse, or was it merely that my attitude had? Even old standbys of prayer and meditation seemed not to help with my empty feelings. I tried desperately to make my house the key to my happiness. I had a lot of work done on it: a yard sprinkler system, automatic gates, a remodeled kitchen. I had plumbing re-done, walls re-painted, workers re-diculous. I think the highlight came when a worker in my kitchen blew his nose into his shirt as I sat ten feet away trying to eat breakfast. I considered a lobotomy in order to remove that gruesome memory.

For whatever reason, I often ended up with work crews that spoke very little English. I'd make what I thought were arrangements to have my trees trimmed; then I'd come home to find them installing a hot tub.

I had an elaborate alarm system put in, which during the first few weeks I managed to trigger so often that the police finally threatened to open a precinct at the end of my driveway. Friends constantly set it off, sometimes in spectacularly dim fashion. "Gee, sorry Ed, I didn't realize busting a window would set off the alarm." Ironically, the alarm system added both security and insecurity simultaneously.

Around this time, I performed a show at the HBO Workspace in Hollywood and was pleasantly surprised when I was approached afterward by a woman with whom I had attended high school. (I don't want to use her real name, which is Pamela, so I'll call her Pam.) She was living in LA and told me she was in charge of our class's upcoming twenty-year reunion. The big event was scheduled to take place in late September at the Andy Warhol Museum, located on the North Side of Pittsburgh. As odd as it seems, Andy Warhol was supposedly from the 'burgh, though I can't confirm that because I never saw him at any of the Steeler games.

"I assume you'll be there, right?" Pam asked.

"Uh, well, I hadn't really planned on going. I'm sort of busy and all," I demurred.

"Oh, nonsense, don't be silly," she cooed. "Everyone wants to see you. Besides, there will be a lot of single women there who I know for a fact would love to chat with you. You mentioned that you're single in your routine. That's true, isn't it?"

"Yes," I stammered. "Unfortunately, it's not all an act."

"Well, good," she replied. "Going to the reunion will be just what you need, Ed. You should hook up with a down-to-earth girl from back home. Not these flaky models out here."

"Yeah, I'm sick of the endless parade of models."

"Seriously, promise you'll come."

I didn't like where this was going. I had only been to

one reunion previously, not counting the time I happened upon three of my former classmates smoking pot in the parking lot of a local tavern. I went to the five-year reunion, but that was largely useless, as every conversation was the same:

"So, what are you doing?"

"Just got out of college, looking for a job. What are you doing?"

"Oh, just got out of college, looking for a job. What are you doing?"

At that time, I had just started doing stand-up for a living, and some of my classmates had asked me if I'd like to perform at the reunion. I told them no thanks; I preferred to kick back and get blasted. Frankly, if there hadn't been an open bar there, I don't think I'd have even gone to the event.

At one point, one of the teachers who was in attendance asked me if I wanted to do a "comedy skit" for everyone. I replied, "Sure, and then maybe you can get up there and teach us a little history." He got my point and didn't ask again.

I thought it odd that teachers were at the five-year reunion in the first place. Not that they weren't welcome, but I couldn't figure out why they'd want to be there. Maybe they were scoping out chicks they had "admired" earlier and had patiently waited for them to become "legal."

I had been in Boston when our class had its eleven-year reunion. That's right, not *ten*-year, but *eleven*-year reunion. Our class never was good at math. Incredibly, the eleven-year reunion was highlighted by the fact that our class was bilked out of thousands of dollars it had paid to a "professional" reunion group that turned out to be a scam. We made national news as gullible yokels, the most attention our school had received since a girl from the class behind mine got engaged to one of the Menendez brothers. This was prior to the little disagreement the boys had with their folks.

I told Pam, "Well, I'll certainly think about attending the reunion. Thanks for coming to my show." We exchanged numbers, and I fled for the safety of my car. As I headed home, however, I found myself actually wondering if Pam could be right. *Maybe a girl from back home is what I need. Though I like LA, I do get homesick at times.* A few days earlier, a friend had called from Pittsburgh to tell me that a local sportscaster had been arrested for offering an undercover officer $20 for oral sex. And all I could think was *Gee, there's another thing I miss about Pittsburgh, the reasonable prices.*

Apparently, there was something in the air that night, because when I got home I got a call from another person I'd gone to high school with. Not really a friend, more of an acquaintance, and I was surprised to hear from him, especially considering the zealous way I guarded the distribution of my phone number. Now, I don't want to embarrass anyone by using any specific names, so I'll just call him Phillip S. Johnson of 12257 Century Avenue, Clearside, PA 15551, (412) 555-9898, PSJwelcher@aol.com. After a bit of small talk, he asked me if I could "help him out." Something about that phrase worried me, and my unease was quickly proven to be justified. He was just a "little short of cash right now," something to do with some court-ordered garnishing of his wages.

Now, God knows I've borrowed money from family and friends plenty of times, especially during the halcyon days of doing stand-up in Massachusetts pizza houses for twenty bucks—if the check didn't bounce. Often, I just worked for free pizza—of course, "That's free pizza with no toppings." As one owner told me, "Toppings are for paying customers." Undoubtedly another magical moment of my life: being talked down to by a guy in a tomato-sauce-splattered apron.

Although I have borrowed from time to time, I was never one for lending money out. Mostly because I never had any to lend. But thanks to good fortune (or, some would argue, bad judgment by people who've hired me), I had managed to accumulate some cash over the previous five years or so. But not nearly as much as many of my friends thought. People assume you're rich if they see you on TV. "Ed, I saw you on *Politically Incorrect*. Wow, you must live in a mansion!" Oh yeah, absolutely. In fact, Hef and the girls often house-sit for me when I decide to jet off to Monaco for the day.

I'm not complaining about the amount of money I make. I guess I only wish I could make what people *think* I make. After all, I do have two hungry mouths to feed: my manager and my agent.

However, I've been really fortunate, so I decided I

could help Phillip. I queried, "How much do you need?" I have since learned that this is a bad question to ask.

"Not much, man. Not much for you." I knew I was in trouble right then.

"How not much?" I asked.

"Five or six thousand."

"Dollars?"

"No, fucking drachma, man."

It's comforting to know that just because one is being asked for a large sum of money doesn't mean one shouldn't be treated with sarcastic contempt. But as I said, I've been blessed lately, so I figured I should do the right thing, which is ask how soon he can pay me back. I was told "very fast," and with that, I sent him off a check. Surely, this would buy me some cosmic goodwill, right?

That goodwill, cosmic or otherwise, came in a hurry, as I had the opportunity to work with Billy Crystal on the Academy Awards that year. The first time I met Billy was when he'd hired me (without knowing me personally) to help with some jokes for a celebrity roast he was hosting. He turned out to be an incredibly nice person, funny, gracious, and generous. Though by this time I had worked with a lot of celebrities, I was really struck by how down to earth a star of his magnitude was.

Billy is married to a lovely woman named Janice, and they have two great kids. Billy and Janice were married way back in the days when he was just a struggling comic. It occurred to me that it must be an incredible experience to be with the same person who was attracted to you when you weren't a celebrity. Billy and

Janice got to ride the show business roller coaster together, the epitome of the "through thick and thin"
which marriages are supposed to endure.

I realized that the fact that I wasn't taking my ride
with the same loyal person from my youth was just as
much my fault as anybody else's. I simply had been too
afraid, or too arrogant, or too "busy," or too suspicious,
or too wrapped up in my own bad habits to sow the
seeds of a healthy relationship.

I was certainly paying the price now, in the currency
of uncertainty and cynicism. For instance, I wanted to
use what fame I had to attract a woman, yet then was
suspicious that she was only with me because of who I
was. I wanted to impress a woman by taking her to the
nicest restaurants and the best resorts, then became
afraid that she was only interested in my money. It was a
lose-lose situation, or at least I thought it was.

Fortunately for me, my career was increasingly becoming a win-win situation, especially when Billy agreed to
host the Academy Awards that year and hired me to be
part of his team.

We scheduled our first Oscars meeting at his house
on a dark, rainy night in January. Though I had been to
his place several times before, I had never driven there
myself. I'm one of those people who, if I'm not the one
driving, could get a ride someplace every day for a year,
yet not be able to tell you exactly how to get there. My
bad sense of direction has become somewhat legendary
among my friends and peers.

During the day, I was doing a long, tough rewrite of a Warner Brothers sitcom and had been pounding coffee all afternoon to make sure I kept my energy alive for the work at Billy's that night. As I drove toward his house in the pouring rain, I got a bit confused as to which street was his. I knew I was in the area, but between the darkness and the bad visibility created by the thunderstorm, I couldn't quite find it.

I started getting nervous, because it was looking like I was going to be late. Also, I stupidly had forgotten to bring Billy's unlisted phone number with me, and if all this wasn't enough, those coffees I'd been drinking were demanding to be released from my body. Hey, what's the worst that could happen? I show up an hour late having pissed myself? Hmm, I guess that *is* pretty bad.

As I desperately backtracked down the same stretch of road for the third time, I realized that even if I were to immediately be magically transported directly to Billy's bathroom, it still wouldn't be fast enough. The only thing left to do was give it the old college try: I'd have to pull over somewhere and whiz outside.

On the positive side, at least it was nighttime. On the negative side, I was in the most posh area of the city, and every time I saw a bit of dark space between houses and pulled over, motion detector lights would blast on, illuminating me completely.

Finally, in total desperation, I pulled my car over to the edge of the street, got out, opened my trunk as if I were looking for something, and slyly unzipped my fly and peed beside my car. The panic I felt was somewhat offset by the sheer relief, but I quickly pictured the horrible scenario of the police coming by, and me explaining that I'm only peeing in the street because I'm on my way to write the Oscars with Billy Crystal. That explanation would probably get me the "Rodney King special" from the LAPD.

Just as I finished up, someone came to the doorway of the house I was in front of and yelled, "Hey!" I yelled, "Hey!" then jumped back in my car and took off. I finally found my way to Billy's and of course didn't have the nerve to tell him what I'd just gone through. I was pretty drenched from being outside, and Billy said, "Wow, it's really raining, huh? You're soaked." All I could say was, "Believe me, it could have been a lot worse."

While working on the Oscars was a lot of pressure, it was also a lot of fun. We had a great crew including David Steinberg, Marc Shaiman, Billy Martin, Jon Macks, Dave Boone, Bruce Vilanch, and Beth Armogida. There were a lot of laughs, on stage and off.

Though everything in my career seemed to go almost exactly as I wanted it to, a vague uneasiness followed me wherever I went. My suspicion grew that no matter how much my career flourished, it would never completely satisfy me.

The reviews that came in after the Oscars in 1997 were overwhelming. We'd scored a huge hit by placing Billy into scenes from each of the best picture nominated films, and it blew everyone away. Billy generously took out a full-page ad thanking us by name. One trade paper opined that "the writers deserve a truckload of Emmys," and I figured we were a shoo-in for another statue. I even made sure I had a nice place on my mantle for it. I was really excited by the likely prospect of winning another one.

Through a highly questionable set of procedural issues, the Oscars were placed in the same Emmy category as shows such as *Late Night with David Letterman* and *Saturday Night Live.* Previously, there had been a category that rightly pitted the awards shows against each other. But for some odd reason, voting categories had been changed, and we were thrown into the apples and oranges nomination bin of hit shows that were nothing like ours. Add to that the fact that we'd broadcast in March and preliminary voting is in July, and we were completely forgotten about. Win the Emmy? Hell, we weren't even *nominated.*

I was bitterly disappointed. In fact, I was devastated, and I knew inside that something was wrong with me for taking it so hard. What had happened to the new, improved perspective I'd acquired after getting sober?

As you've probably figured out, I'm a very ambitious person. Ambition can be a good thing, but like many good things, it can easily become a bad thing. When harnessed properly, ambition causes a person to work hard, to use their natural abilities while simultaneously cultivating abilities that don't come as easily. Ambition, at its best, is what drives mankind to develop great medical breakthroughs, technological advances, and artistic masterpieces. At its worst, though, ambition can be the chief cause of greed, dishonesty, and ultimately, numbing unhappiness.

It's something I personally grapple with every day. When is my ambition healthy, and when isn't it so? The best indicator seems to be how I'm feeling inside. When I'm doing my part, which is to do the work in front of me to the best of my ability, I feel good, regardless of the ultimate results, which I, of course, don't control anyway. When I'm attempting to overstep my responsibilities, trying to do more than my part, such as fretting over the results of my work, desperately scheming to make events unfold as I wish them to, then I feel anxious and ungrateful. These feelings are a clear indication that I've strayed over the line into the unhealthy aspects of ambition.

Enjoying the process of whatever one is doing, instead of trying to control the results, seems to be a basic prerequisite for keeping some sense of happiness. As with most keys to serenity, however, this is much easier said than done.

When I first got sober, I lived in a very small studio apartment in Boston, but I was content and seemed to have all the room I needed. When I moved to a bigger apartment in Boston, I initially was concerned about having enough things to fill it. However, I eventually found myself with an apartment that was not only filling up in a hurry, but actually seemed to not have enough room. When I moved to a bigger apartment in LA, I figured, *Surely I've got all the space I need now.* But that was followed by a move to yet another, more spacious apartment, and I soon found that I seemed to once again be pressed for space. When I bought a house, I figured my space needs were now set for life, but as you might guess, after a year or so, I found that I "needed" a bigger house, as my little house was too cramped. This brought me to my present, even bigger house, which, amazingly enough, seems to not be as spacious as I thought it was when I bought it. I somehow seem to expand to the size of wherever it is I'm living.

This also is what my life seems to do. When I got sober, all my true needs were taken care of, and I felt I really had everything I needed to be happy. Everything to come was just gravy. And when I moved to LA and won an Emmy, I felt certainly this was all I needed to finally feel accomplished. But interestingly enough, I found myself lusting after yet more Emmys, and more success, just as I'd desired more and more space wherever I lived.

This is not to say it's wrong to want to accomplish things, or wrong to want a nice house, or wrong to strive to better one's life. It's the attitude that goes with it that is of concern. One must appreciate what one has and not feel that one's happiness is contingent exclusively on whether or not one is able to take that next "upward step," be it in career, relationships, housing, or whatever.

I have to constantly remind myself to stop and taste the gravy.

Dating?
I Do It Religiously

While I was usually able to get back to the "gravy" as far as my career was concerned, I seemed unable to get past the bitterness and cynicism caused by my breakup with Rita. I struggled to find an explanation of why it still hurt so much and why it continued to inflict so much emotional damage.

Admittedly, Rita and I had too many moments together that weren't very pleasant, perhaps because we shared some of the same character flaws. For most relationships that fail, the culprit is irreconcilable differences. For Rita and me, it may have been irreconcilable similarities.

We both hated to talk directly about what was bothering us, a shared defect that would ultimately break us apart forever.

We both tended to *catastrophize* situations, and while

my complaining was usually at least comedic, it still caused us to incite each other into unnecessary states of frustration. For instance, when we were waiting to board an airplane and there was a delay, I'd get impatient, and she would, too, and before you knew it, we'd provoked each other into complete and total aggravation. Naturally, this made us extremely popular not only with the flight crew, but with our fellow passengers as well.

The fact that we were both in the entertainment business also turned out to be a problem. Though our jobs were completely different, hers dealing entirely with technical production aspects and mine dealing with creative aspects, we worked on some of the same shows and knew many of the same people. But for some reason, she felt that I didn't respect her side of the business. This was completely untrue. I respect the hard work and long hours and creativity that goes into all aspects of a television or film project, and I mentioned this to her quite often. But it didn't matter what I said, because her perception was that I had little regard for her work. With Rita, her perception was definitely reality. Instead of viewing us as a team, she saw us as competitors, something I never understood.

I remember once I came home with what I thought was good news. I had signed a big contract to write a television pilot. When I told her what I was being paid, she looked angry and pointed out how it was much more than she was making on her current project.

Her reaction hurt and baffled me. Here I was thinking she'd be thrilled, because after all, the benefits of my good fortune were going to be reaped by her and our future family. But she somehow saw it as an insult, an invalidation of her own work.

It's not like all our moments together were like that. Indeed, when I first met and fell in love with Rita, I truly thought I'd gotten past my fear of involvement, and felt that there really was a perfect person for me. I was convinced that we were "destined" to be together. She was beautiful, and smart, and funny. I was especially impressed by Rita's intellect and creativity. She was an accomplished flute player and did a lot of needlepoint (which maybe should have been a clue that she might later "blow me off," then "stick it to me"). She was everything I could ask for, including a terrific listener.

One night, I came home freaking out after having a terrible show in front of some people I really wanted to impress. I was inconsolable. At least, I thought I was, until Rita held me in her arms and assured me that everything was going to be okay. She told me that she believed in me and that I could, and would, accomplish everything I wanted to, if I just kept the faith. I'll never forget how comforting she was, and I remember thinking, *Wow, if there ever was any doubt this is the woman for me, it's been erased right here, right now.*

That is exactly what made our breakup so devastating to me. I'd briefly allowed myself to believe relationships weren't completely futile pursuits that would inevitably end in pain, but it turned out my cynical inner voice had been right all along. I don't think I've ever been more sorry to have my opinions proven correct.

I suppose I should have been able to cherish those good times, as so many people do after they break up and get on with their lives. However, I found myself unable, or unwilling, to do so. I found it extremely difficult to move on. In fact, I was filled with nothing but regret, mostly for having put myself in a position of vulnerability that would allow me to be hurt so deeply, especially when I had taken such great pains in the past to avoid doing that very thing. These unbecoming feelings of self-pity and remorse were clearly a case of spilled gravy.

Though I was doing my best to date and remain open to the possibility of another woman in my life, in the back of my mind I was convinced that the one area of my life that would never work out was relationships.

As usual, thank goodness for the distraction that was my career. One Friday night, I worked at my favorite LA nightclub, the Comedy & Magic Club in Hermosa Beach. Similar to Catch back in Boston, which sadly now is closed, the C&M (there always seems to be a cool people's version of a club name) is a creatively supportive environment. This is largely due to its dedicated owner, Mike Lacey. He's made sure that it has the kind of class not seen in most comedy venues, and thus it's no surprise that his club is regularly frequented by Leno, Shandling, Seinfeld, and, of course, Driscoll.

I was having a great set but then made the mistake of doing a joke about an impending military showdown between two impoverished nations. "A war between Pakistan and India? Well, you know it sure won't be a food fight. Nobody's eaten in either country for the last twenty years." Some in the crowd moaned in disapproval, and I can't say I was completely surprised.

Now, of course starvation isn't funny, and that's kind of the point. Will my tears rid the world of this horrible condition? If so, please let me know and I'll bawl my eyes out into every container they can bring me, and we can use it to grow enough crops for every man, woman, and child on the planet. A comedian deals with these issues onstage, at least this comedian does, because silence in the face of these tough realities of life never really rested very well with me. And what makes it worse is that often when people gather together as an audience, they feel obligated to develop this pseudo-conscience about which topics are appropriate fodder for humor and which are taboo. This would be fine except that you know these are the same people who were e-mailing Columbine and tsunami jokes to each other at work immediately following those tragedies. It's a ridiculous double standard, and I see it all the time.

I once wrote an article for *George* magazine in which I fictitiously quoted Bob Dole as saying, "Now, thanks to Viagra, I've got something else to hold in my hand besides a pen." I received a vicious piece of anonymous hate mail asking, "What kind of horrible person writes horrible things about another person, you asshole?" The answer would seem to be, nameless people who are not in touch with their own irony.

Despite the "food fight" joke, I managed to win the whole C&M crowd back by the end of my show, and actually had the courage to leave via the front door when suddenly someone grabbed my arm. It was Pam, our fearless reunion organizer. "Are you a comedy fan, or are you just stalking me?" I asked, mostly in jest. She assured me she liked comedy, "As well as whatever it is that you do, Ed." I laughed at her good-natured put-down. Then she dropped the big one. She asked me if I'd like to do a "comedy bit" at the reunion. "Uh, gee, uh, I'm flattered and all," I lied, "but, you know, I think I'd rather just attend and visit with everyone."

I wasn't being snobbish. I just figured I had nothing to gain and everything to lose by attempting to do stand-up at a reunion. I didn't need to be humiliated in front of my classmates. My prom had covered that more than adequately. I had received many nice notes over the years from people who had seen me on television or read about me someplace, which I really appreciated. But I figured these people didn't need to be distracted by me spouting off into a microphone while they were busy trying to squint at each other's name tags without getting caught.

But Pam kept pressing me, and finally I said, "Well, I suppose I could say a few words; let me think about it."

The next day was Saturday, a day to relax for most people, but I knew it might not be so peaceful for me, as I was expecting a delivery. Earlier in the week, I had purchased two beds and was told they would be delivered between 9 a.m. and 5 p.m. I love the way companies are so incredibly vague about their time. I wanted to say,

"Great, I'll pay you sometime between March and December." But I kept quiet, knowing enough not to give the Toss 'N Turn Bed Company any further excuse to screw with my order. I had a function to attend that night and was hopeful the beds would arrive sooner rather than later so I could leave in time.

Finally, at 5:30 that evening, with no delivery people in sight, I called the company to say that I was still waiting. The owner snapped at me: "It's just a window, sir. Not an exact time." I guess it really was obnoxious of me to hold people to an eight-hour time frame. I told the owner, "I think eight hours should be enough to deliver two beds. I could have built my own in less time than that." "It's just a window, pal." Great. Now I've been downgraded from "sir" to "pal." How large a window did they need? If I'd had one that big, I'd have jumped out of it and ended the misery right then and there. When I insisted he check with his drivers, he discovered that they were attempting to deliver my beds to the wrong address. Of course, the owner apologized by saying, "Okay, I told them the right address and they'll get there when they get there." Oh, please, don't overdo it. I hate when people kiss my ass like that.

Since I had to wait for the beds to arrive, I was now going to be late for the function I planned to attend. I had read in a local church bulletin about an "Entertainment Singles Fellowship," a group of single Catholic professionals in the entertainment industry. Many people read some of the sick stuff I write and wonder how I reconcile it with being a churchgoer. Well, it's my belief that God gave me a twisted sense of humor for a reason. Perhaps just to bother those with no sense of humor at all.

As with a lot of people, my religious leanings and attendance at religious services took a labyrinthine path. As a child, I thought religion was kind of neat, though church was often boring. As a teenager, I saw it as an inconvenient obligation, when there were so many cool things to do, to have to spend a whole hour (!) of my week in a church. As a young adult in my twenties, while still keeping my belief in God, I rationalized that I didn't really need to go to church. After all, I was a pretty good person, and besides, I was extremely busy trying to build a life and a career. But as I got into my thirties, and especially when I quit drinking, I found myself searching for answers as to the greater meaning of life and found comfort in the quiet beauty and sense of community that church offers.

I'll admit there are times when I have some serious doubts about God. Not about His existence, but about who or what He really is, and about exactly what He does or doesn't do. It used to make me feel incredibly guilty. But a priest friend of mine told me that all people of faith have doubts at some time, that it's only natural. I went to this same priest for counseling after my breakup with Rita, and I said, "Relationships are really hard, Father." And he said, "No shit, that's why I'm a priest."

To me, it's simply not logical to believe there's no God. How else to explain the incredible "coincidences" we all encounter nearly every day? How else to explain the birds, the trees, the dandelions, the chemicals I spray on the dandelions to kill them?

So I'm a believer, albeit a shaky one some days. I'll continue to pursue and analyze spirituality. I suppose the very fact that I believe in God in the face of un-answerable questions and frightening uncertainties is the very definition of faith. Even in confusing times, spirituality *has* to be better than materialism. At the very least, it doesn't require anywhere near the storage space.

As I waited impatiently for the delivery guys, I became more and more intrigued about attending the Entertain-ment Singles group. I figured it would be a safe haven in which to talk with others about mutual struggles with unscrupulous people in our field and to learn how to re-sist agendas we might consider morally questionable. Plus, I might actually meet a chick.

The beds finally arrived, and after the unapologetic workers left, I headed out to the function, to see if I could possibly find some use for the beds, other than sleeping.

I knew I was in trouble when I first arrived at the singles fellowship meeting and the guy in charge hugged me. Now, you'll have to excuse me, and it's probably my "issue," but I haven't hugged my own father since I was five, so the last thing I want to do is put my arms around some sweaty stranger. I sure was caught off guard, and in fact my first instinct when he hugged me was to knee him in the groin. I resisted that urge, but did go with my second instinct, which was to check and make sure my wallet wasn't gone.

When the meeting finally got under way, the entire group consisted of five men and one frightened-looking woman. Most of the guys had that glazed look in their eyes that one only sees in religious zealots and heroin addicts. We sat and the discussion began. So much for my hope to have a genuine debate of issues facing Catholics in show business. Instead, I was treated to bitter people complaining because they were asked to audition with a script that contained the word "shit." I finally said, "Hey, most scripts are nothing but shit to begin with anyway, so what's all the fuss?" Only one person laughed, but fortunately for me it was the woman. Her name was Sarah, and during the break we chatted. She was smart and extremely pretty, and shared the same opinion of the function as I did. I asked for her phone number, and we made a date for the following weekend.

When I picked her up at her apartment, I noticed her perfume and told her how nice it was. She replied, "Funny you should say that. When I bought it, the lady at the store said, 'This scent drives men crazy,' and I didn't believe her, but the first night I wore it, six guys asked me out!"

On the drive to the restaurant, she told me of an ex-boss of hers who'd always been asking her out even though he was married, and that she'd always refused.

Then, he'd called her that afternoon because he'd just been divorced, and asked her out again.

When we arrived at our dining destination, she went into a lengthy story about how when she'd been a coat-check girl, she was always getting hit on by guys.

Okay, this was getting freaky. What was the purpose of these stories? Were they supposed to make me jealous? Or make me feel extremely lucky to be out with someone so incredibly desirable that men were throwing themselves at her feet? Whatever the point behind these tales, they were definitely getting on my nerves.

When we ordered our meal, Sarah talked about how once she'd been out with a guy and when he'd gone to use the restroom, their waiter had asked her out. I said, "Well fortunately, I've worn my Depends undergarments, so no bathroom trips will be necessary for me!"

When our dinners arrived, she began talking about our church and, without thinking, I cut her off with, "Wait, don't tell me. You went to midnight Mass, and the Pope showed up and asked you out." She gave me a strange look. "Why did you say that?" she asked.

"Well, I'm sorry, but you've been going on and on about how everyone asks you out all the time. Why are you telling me this? You're obviously beautiful. I'm sold, so what's the deal? It's like you're trying to convince yourself you're desirable or something."

She said nothing for a moment, then said, "I'm sorry. You're not the first to complain about this. I've been working on it with my psychiatrist." I instantly regretted having said anything. I told her, "Hey, I'm not really complaining. I'm just confused about it, that's all." Sarah said, "Well, my therapist says it's a common trait among women who come from households where the father left. My dad skipped out on us when I was five."

My mind went immediately to Tiffany, the "French fry" woman. She was very pretty as well, and she also had a bit of the "everyone asks me out" syndrome, if not quite to Sarah's extent. And Tiffany's father also had abandoned her family. Wow, amazing stuff. But then the thought occurred to me, my family was still together, so what was my excuse for being such a goof?

I ended up making Sarah laugh about it all, and when I dropped her off at her apartment, I apologized again for my Pope comment. She said, "Hey, he'd forgive you, so I guess I can, too." She was nice, but we both agreed we probably weren't a good match.

The next evening, I sat by myself in a favorite neighborhood diner. Despite the fact that we'd decided not to pursue any sort of relationship, I actually felt pretty good about the experience with Sarah and how I'd handled it. After all, I hadn't gotten sarcastic, or defensive. Okay, I'd been a bit sarcastic, but at least I had apologized for doing so. For me, that was some real growth. I was treading dangerously close to becoming a mature adult. If I wasn't careful, I might become marriage material after all.

I watched a young couple at an adjacent table as they tried to eat while simultaneously corralling their young children, a boy and a girl who both must have been about five years old. I started fantasizing about what it would be like to have children. These kids were so cute, and I started imagining what my own children might look like someday. I pictured myself teaching them how to play catch in the backyard. This pleasant daydream was interrupted when the little boy hit me in the face with his dinner roll.

"I'm so sorry," his mother said.

"It's okay; I was just going to ask the waiter for more bread," I told her. Overall, the children were really well behaved, and I couldn't help but notice that both the woman and her husband seemed to have a natural touch with their kids. If only all parents did.

I love kids, I really do. I get a kick out of it when I'm working in my yard and neighborhood children stop by and actually say, "Whatcha doing, Mister D?" Quite a Mayberry moment. I'm glad they like me, instead of thinking I'm one of those old guys living alone who steals soccer balls that end up in my flowerbeds. I can imagine them standing out in the street whispering among themselves: "Don't ever go over there. That's old man Driscoll's place. *They say he never married.*"

At the risk of being called curmudgeonly, and thus having to look the word up in the dictionary, I have to say: kids that aren't your own can often be quite irritating. First of all, parents should stop letting their kids answer the telephone. In fact, they shouldn't be allowed anywhere near the phone until they're old enough to pay the phone bills. There are few things in life more annoying than when you call someone regarding something really important and/or urgent and find that you have to slip into Fred Rogers mode because a two-year-old is running interference at the other end of the receiver. I know parents are trying to impress people with how smart their toddlers are by having them field calls, but if you really want to impress me, have the child drive you to work.

Plus, even when you do get to actually talk to the adult you're trying to reach, they're always so easily distracted by their children. I always feel like I'm intruding. They will have entire conversations with the kid while I patiently wait to finish my unimportant story about my CAT-scan results.

Kids aren't easy to handle in person, either. Once they get mobile, they really become a danger. I know that every item they get their hands on is destined for either my crotch or my skull. I'm more at ease in a room with a drunk guy swinging a hatchet than near a toddler holding a Wiffle bat. Their toys even seem intentionally manufactured to do the maximum amount of damage to the nearest adult. "Hey, Uncle Eddie, check out my new Fisher-Price Eye-Gouger."

Nobody ever said raising kids is easy. It's an awesome job and an awesome responsibility, requiring incredible patience. Kids are difficult and costly and draining, and . . . I can't wait to have some of my own! What can I say? Many instincts defy logic. But I'd better be careful, because I won't be physically capable of offspring if my nephew gives me one more shot in the nuts with that Spider-Man action figure. Although the way it was going with my social life, it appeared as though it really wouldn't matter anyway.

When I got home from the diner, I brought in the mail and noticed an envelope reading "Important Reunion Information." I assumed it was for me, though it was addressed to "Ted" Driscoll. Months had gone by and I hadn't heard back from Pam, so I figured I was safe as far as having to perform at the function. But to my horror, when I opened the envelope and read the invitation, right there in big letters were the words "Special comedy routine by Ed Driscoll!"

I immediately called Pam and asked her what the deal was with the reunion. She sputtered, "What do you mean; didn't you get your invitation?" She then sheepishly told me that she'd meant to get back to me to make sure I'd do it, but she ran out of time and the invites had to go to press and she had started a new project at work and the dog ate her homework and . . . Well, what could I do except agree to do it? I told her I was a little embarrassed about having my name splashed across the invites and was worried people would think I was being egomaniacal or insisting on performing there or something. She assured me that nobody would think that, and I let her go when my other line clicked in. It was my friend Jim from Pittsburgh, who began the conversation with, "Wow man, you've gone Hollywood. Did you insist on them billing you in big letters like that? You'd think you'd be modest enough to just attend and not have to show off in front of everyone."

The other thing on the invitation that jumped out at me was the cost: $96 per person. Ninety-six dollars? Were they billing us in advance for damage they thought we were going to do? I could buy every work of art Andy Warhol ever made for less than that. To make things even more torturous, I feared some people would think that a big chunk of the money was going to me for my little "performance," just another hellish false assumption that I'd have to clear up every time I was asked about it.

I felt a bit ridiculous that I was so concerned, not only with how my performance went over, but with how my old classmates thought of me. I was absurdly obsessed with how a small group of acquaintances, many of whom I hadn't seen or talked to in twenty years, might perceive me. Horrible self-absorption at its finest.

Though by many standards I was successful, both professionally and personally, I naturally chose to focus on the ways in which I felt I wasn't. After all, I mused, I'm not a big star, I don't have my own television show, I don't have a girlfriend, I'm not a parent, my hair's thinning, others have achieved a lot more by this age, a lot of people make more money and have bigger houses and have better connections and . . . uh oh, I seem to have spilled my gravy once again.

I'm not proud of these thought processes, and they occur more frequently than I'd like to admit. The only consistency in my thinking is my inconsistency. Sometimes I have a tremendous sense of priorities and gratitude, and other times I can be ridiculously petty and un-appreciative. I recall walking down the street in Boston one afternoon, very upset because my Rotisserie base-ball results had just come in and my team had fallen into last place. As I grumpily made my way through the lunchtime crowd, I saw a blind woman with a seeing-eye dog that was limping. I was overcome with compassion, for both the woman and the poor dog, who obviously had something wrong with his foot but bravely contin-ued to serve his dependent master. I felt deep shame for allowing myself to actually waste one minute of life being upset over some fantasy baseball results. I wish I could say that was the last time I wasted energy brood-ing over something so meaningless, but unfortunately, it wasn't. However, I often think of the woman and her dog, and it actually does help bring me back to reality. I remain incredibly touched by that image, and I've prob-ably offered more prayers on their behalf than I have on behalf of my own relatives. It's strange how fleeting mo-ments and images in life can so profoundly affect us.

I pondered the reality that I can't control what others think about me, nor is it my right to even attempt to do so. In this life, as long as I work hard, and I'm as good a person as I can be, I'm doing my part. Besides, I realized that nobody is really spending their time thinking about me. They're thinking about what others are thinking about them! I determined to do my utmost to simply enjoy the festivities.

Since I was now officially committed to perform at the reunion, I figured, maybe I could just put together a bit of reminiscing about goofy stuff that happened our senior year. I asked Pam if she would send out questionnaires to our classmates to see what they were doing now. I thought we could have them share some of their favorite moments from school days that I could talk about in my routine. In other words, let's have everyone else write my material for me. The response, of course, was overwhelming. Over seven people took the time to send in their favorite moments. In another sparkling example of our school's educational prowess, the questionnaires contained the line "Use separate sheet *of* needed."

Chapter

❈ 8 ❈

Cooking with Pam

I do a lot of "punch-up" work, that is, adding jokes and scenes to television shows and movies. This is usually done in collaboration with other writers and producers in a conference area referred to as "the writers' room." Most of the time, it's a pretty fun job, but it can be a lot more grueling than many people realize. The writers' room, especially on sitcoms, is mostly a torture chamber, without the blood. (Though I've seen blood drawn there, too.) Sitting in a small room with eight to ten other people for ten to fifteen hours a day may not seem so tough, but as one writer likes to point out, it's like flying to Europe every day, without getting to do any sightseeing.

I sure run into some interesting people on these jobs. The stereotype that everyone in Los Angeles sees themselves as an actor, writer, director, or all three, is essentially true. This isn't necessarily a bad thing. I'm all for people following their dreams and setting their goals high. But there are proper ways to do so, which means there are improper ways as well.

Once, when I was working on a show for ABC, something had gone wrong with my computer and a technician came to my office to fix it. I left him to his work for a while, then later came back and asked, "Hey, how's it going?" He said, "Oh, good." I then noticed he had the script I was currently working on open, and he was jotting something down in it. "What are you doing?" I asked incredulously. He looked at me and nonchalantly said, "I'm just writing down a couple of suggestions for the script." As I stared at him in complete astonishment, he went on to pitch his jokes to me. As you might expect, they made no sense whatsoever.

I couldn't believe what was happening. If he wanted to be a writer and had asked me to look at some of his samples, I would have been glad to. But this was incredible even by Hollywood standards. Finally, I managed to sputter out, "Did you fix my computer?" He said, "Oh, yeah." I said, "Well, thanks, and could you order me a moving van?"

He gave me a confused look. "What for?"

"To pick up your balls and take them out of my office."

He got my point and left. When the line producer found out what had happened, she wanted to fire him immediately, but I asked her not to do that. I actually felt sorry for anyone who could be so oblivious.

Writers are often disrespected, or unappreciated, or

both, but not always. There are many stars who highly value good writing. A guy like Drew Carey often sits in on the writing sessions and genuinely appreciates and contributes to the process. In short, he "gets it." So does Garry Shandling, who began his illustrious career as a writer, and is still a damn good one. But often, stars of shows have absolutely no clue what preparing the script entails. When I was working on a show that shall remain nameless (and virtually unwatched, as well), the star announced he'd like to sit in and pitch his ideas during the next roundtable. He lasted almost an hour, until he realized that these writers had to spend all that time in the room actually writing, while he could be back home by his pool learning his lines for the next day. It was an easy choice for him, and we never saw him anywhere but the stage again.

I came dragging home from yet another late night of punching up scenes for a movie at Warner Brothers studios when I noticed that I had a message on my answering machine. Since I hadn't taped any ball games, it was safe to listen to the message. It was Pam.

"Hi, Ed. I just wanted to make sure you were all set for your big performance next week. Thanks so much for doing it, and don't forget, there are a lot of single girls who are looking forward to seeing you. Who knows, you could find your future wife there. It just might be someone you least expect. See ya."

As most neurotics do, I began to look for the *real* meaning behind her message. Why did she keep harping on this "single girl" thing? And what did she mean by "least expect"? Then, it hit me. She's talking about herself! She is the one who wants to hook up with me! After all, she went out of her way every time I talked to her to mention that she was single, and she was from "back home," just as she said I "needed a woman from back home." And she did seem to pop up at all of my performances, and . . . wow, this was an unexpected development. I had never thought of her that way. She's cute, and smart, and nice, really perfect girlfriend material. Man, why hadn't I thought about her before? And how could I have been so oblivious to her feelings for me? Here she'd been dropping as many hints as she possibly could have without actually coming right out and screaming, "Ask me out, you jerk!" And even if she had done that, I still probably wouldn't have caught on.

This epiphany certainly put a new spin on the whole reunion deal. And I had thought there was pressure before, when I was just worried about how my jokes would do! Not only did I have to impress my classmates; I had to continue to impress Pam. I realized that I now needed to be in top form, mentally and physically. It was time for a crash course in self-improvement. I could hear the unmistakable melody of the training music from *Rocky* soaring through my head.

Where to start? Well, I guess at the top, literally. My hair. Truth be told, I was already dying my graying hair, mostly to look younger on television. I didn't tell people when I initially had it done, and the first time I appeared on the tube with my hair darkened, my ball-busting pal

Turk called from Pittsburgh and said, "Hey, they must use weird lighting on that show, because I couldn't see any gray hair."

It wasn't the color that concerned me as much as the fact that it was thinning out. I hadn't really given it much thought until just the week before. Billy Crystal cast me in a small role in his film *My Giant.* I played the obnoxious emcee at a wedding. If you don't remember that character from the film, well, you shouldn't, because my scene ended up on the cutting room floor. When I was in the makeup chair before filming, the hairstylist looked at my skull, then started shaking this little can of fake hair onto my head. I was puzzled and asked why he was doing that. "Oh, I'm just filling it in a little on the top here." *Hmm,* I thought. I knew I'd lost a tiny bit of hair, but certainly it couldn't be that significant.

When he was still shaking the can over me five minutes later, I became alarmed. "Is it really that bald up there?" I asked in a panic. "Well, I've seen worse," he offered diplomatically.

Of course, being the obsessive person that I am, the minute I got home I rigged up an intricate system of mirrors in order to thoroughly view the back of my head. Sure enough, I was losing it. (The hair, I mean.) I started using Rogaine, which helped. I had to get used to it, though. Twice a day I had to stand in front of a mirror and use what appears to be a turkey baster to place the drops on top of my head. For the first few weeks, most of the Rogaine just dripped right off my skull, so that my head had absolutely no new hair, but my back and ass looked like Sasquatch. I finally got the hang of it, thank goodness. I didn't want to have to start using styling gel on my butt.

Next on the self-improvement checklist was "Lose some weight!" I went on the Barry Sears Zone Diet. It was hard. All the weight I gain always goes right to my gut. If the weight would just distribute itself evenly, I wouldn't care. I wouldn't mind if I was a well-formed fat guy; that would be okay. But all my weight goes right to my stomach. So if I'm not careful, I end up with skinny legs, skinny arms, and no shoulders, but a big, fat gut. It's that starving, Third World refugee look that women find irresistible. All I'm missing is flies buzzing around me.

I love to eat terrible food. What can I say? Meat, cheese, bread, pasta, anything fattening that I can jam down my gullet with the zeal of Shamu ending a hunger strike. I like to go to "all-you-can-eat" buffets, where I always feel obligated to get what I perceive to be my money's worth. For a month afterward all I can wear is maternity clothing. And this talk of possible chemical warfare from terrorists? Hah! I eat fast food. The chemicals in my body will kill anything those wacky terrorists can toss my way. I've ingested more hazardous, man-made compounds at lunch than Al Qaeda carries in its entire arsenal. These are weapons of ASS destruction.

Truthfully, I had never worried much about those eating habits, despite many passionate pleas from Ahmos to drop a few pounds. I call the Barry Sears Zone a "diet," but it's really not a diet. It's more about changing how and what you eat. It's not a temporary fix to enable one to slip into one's corduroy pants by the weekend, but a total overhaul of one's eating habits. But let's face it, if you're not ready to change your eating lifestyle, you're not ready. A few months prior, a friend of mine had tried to get me interested in dietary health by giving me a book on nutrition. I poured cheese on the book and ate it. However, with the impending reunion, and after seeing a photo of myself looking like someone who needed to be adopted by Dick Gregory, I finally decided that I had to get in shape.

"The Zone" is often referred to as 40-30-30, which I believe stands for "I'm almost *forty;* I have to drop *thirty* pounds; God, I wish I were *thirty* again." I discovered one can actually eat pretty well staying within the confines of the zone; you just can't swallow whole six-piece dinners from Colonel Sanders.

Besides diet, there's another half to the equation, the half nobody really wants, the Garfunkel to diet's Simon: exercise. I remember sitting on my couch in front of the television one night, eating pizza and washing it down with a glass of pancake batter. An ad for one of those home gym systems appeared on the screen, featuring some guy more cut than a blind fencer telling me, "This could be your body." And all I thought was, I could order this equipment and work out every day to look like him, but it really would be simpler to have a doctor graft my head onto that guy's body.

I used to belong to a health club back in Pittsburgh, which of course means that I paid several thousand dollars to drop by twice a month and stand at the side of the running track watching the women's aerobics class. It's nice belonging to a gym when you have a friend visiting who wants to work out, but bringing a guest to one's health club can sometimes turn into a dicey situation. Once, when my friend Walt was in town, I took him to my gym. Walt spent the entire time trying to get some exercise while staff members harangued him mercilessly about purchasing a membership for himself. You'd think they'd have backed off after he vomited in the whirlpool, but one employee actually told him, "See, if you joined and worked out every day, that wouldn't happen." I told Walt he should join and come in and puke in a different section of the club every day. I bet they'd revoke his membership and even give him a refund after a week or so of that.

I figured the best chance for me to work out consistently, other than unexpectedly being drafted into the armed forces, was to purchase home equipment. My reasoning was this: the more obstacles to working out I put in my way, the easier it would be to find excuses not to. By joining a gym, that would mean I'd have to get dressed, get in my car, drive to the club, find parking, walk into the club, discover I'd forgotten my membership card, drive back home, get the card, drive back to the gym, sign in, drive back home again because I had to go to the bathroom and I hate using public restrooms, then drive back to the club to work out. But if I bought a treadmill and some weights and put them in my den, I'd have to walk past them every morning, which would make me feel too guilty, so I'd have to work out.

I purchased a treadmill at my local Sears, a deluxe model that features a piece of cheesecake dangling on a string in front of you as incentive to keep running. I then purchased a series of dumbbells adding up to hundreds and hundreds of pounds. The salesman actually asked me if I could carry the weights out to my car by myself. Hey, if I could do that, I wouldn't need them, now would I?

Ahmos assured me that if I maintained an exercise and diet regimen, I would be amazed at my progress. I threw myself into weightlifting with reckless abandon. After several weeks, I knew I had developed muscles. Not because any were visible, but because I could feel that several were pulled and possibly torn. Perfect. No gain, all pain. It got discouraging, but as I had theorized, it was hard for me to just walk past this equipment every day. It was hard, but I'm proud to say that I learned to do it. In fact, I worked myself up to the point where not only could I ignore the weights entirely, but I could actually lie down on the motionless treadmill and eat a box of donuts, guilt-free. Now that's progress.

Finally, I thought, screw this. It's not like I'm grossly overweight, and Pam didn't seem to mind it as far as I could tell.

I checked off the items on my "Operation Pam/

Reunion" list. Hair color? Check. Hair thickness? Check. Waistline thickness? Unfortunately, check. Aura of success and confidence? Uh, check, I guess . . . mostly, you know . . . yeah, that's a check, sure.

So what was left? Oh yes, the routine I'd be doing. As usual in my life, that part was the easiest; lots of material came to me without even thinking too much about it. If only the other areas of my life were as effortless, I'd be . . . I'd be somebody else, I guess. But for better or worse, I'd be attending the reunion as myself, which seemed good enough for Pam, and, thus, was good enough for me.

Chapter

✹9✹

Reunion:
Back to the Future

Iboarded the plane for Pittsburgh and decided I'd look over the material I planned to use at the reunion. As I perused my notes, I had the unsettling feeling that the guy sitting next to me was reading over my shoulder. I shot him a look, and he asked, "Hey, are those jokes?" I replied, *"No hablo Ingles,"* then put my headphones on, not even bothering to plug them into anything. Fortunately, after eyeing me suspiciously for a moment, my nosy neighbor turned his attention to bothering the person sitting on the other side of him.

As I reviewed the material, I noted which routines Pam had already seen. Since she'd been to several of my shows already, I wanted to demonstrate my versatility by not repeating any of the jokes she'd seen previously. After all, if I looked good, it would make her, as architect of the evening, look good as well. Who knows, if I had a great show, she might be so impressed that she'd practically throw herself at me.

Was it really possible that Pam was the one that fate had been guiding me to for all these years? Could someone I'd gone to school with as a youngster and not even dated actually become one of the chief figures in my life?

Hey, this whole reunion might be a lot more fun than I'd originally thought it would be. Certainly it would be interesting to see how people had changed, physically and otherwise, in the last two decades. What had they gone through, what obstacles had they overcome, what hurdles had they found impossible to navigate? And, at the very least, Phillip, the guy I lent money to months earlier, was scheduled to be there, and maybe he'd pay me back. I knew I couldn't count on that, however, because over the past few years, I've learned that different people have different concepts of what it means to "lend." To me, when I ask someone to "lend" me money, there is the clear and proper assumption that I will pay the money back. I've always paid back my debts (well, I did stiff the Columbia Record Club once, but I distinctly remember sending back the card informing them I didn't want the Little River Band cassette). But to many people, "lend me money" no more implies paying back than "lend me a Kleenex" implies giving that back.

When I landed in Pittsburgh, my friend Steve was waiting for me at the gate. He was clutching a copy of our senior yearbook, telling me he thought it might be a good source to use in my routine. I waved my notes at him and said, "I actually have all my jokes right here," to which he said, "I'm surprised they let you on the plane with those bombs." Ah, there's nothing like friends to keep one grounded. Steve and I made plans to ride together to the reunion the next day, and he dropped me off at my folks' place in the old neighborhood.

It was great to see my parents again, and it was fun to be back in my old bedroom. My folks had kept the room largely the same since I'd left, with yellowing posters of Bruce Springsteen still decorating the walls and a well-worn Steelers trash can sitting in the corner next to an old stereo. I teased my mom that it was like an "Ed Driscoll teenage tribute museum," to which she replied, "I guess if you want to make it authentic, you should throw your dirty clothes all over the floor."

My dad and I watched a Pirates game on television that evening, and during the seventh inning stretch, he started squirming a bit as though he wanted to tell me something. I asked, "What is it, Dad?" He hemmed and hawed a bit, then told me that he just wanted me to know how proud he was of me and all that I had accomplished. I was completely stunned, not because of what he said, but because he actually said it. My father and I have always had mutual love and admiration for each other, but it's gone largely unspoken because, well, guys don't speak about that stuff.

The following day, Steve swung by the house to pick me up, and my mom answered the door. Steve asked her, "Can Eddie come to the reunion, or does he have diarrhea?"

We picked up Turk, Jim, and John, my old grade-school prank buddy, and headed for the North Side. After careful consideration, I had decided not to tell my friends about the situation with Pam. I figured they'd know soon enough, and I certainly didn't need them to regress back to our behavior in high school. Back then, whenever there was a suspicion of romance between a girl and one of our friends, we'd always feel obliged to make things as difficult and awkward as possible. This included mature things like making faces behind the girl as she talked to our buddy or giving her misinformation about him, such as his continual struggle to overcome bedwetting. No, I definitely didn't need their "help" on this one.

We arrived at the Andy Warhol Museum and stepped out of Steve's SUV, or more accurately, we jumped out. I was just thankful I didn't snap an ankle. Suddenly, a gleaming Jaguar peeled into the parking lot, turning everyone's heads. A guy dressed to the nines stepped out. Imagine my surprise when I saw that it was none other than my deadbeat pal, Phillip.

"Hey, Phil, how's it going?" I called to him.

"Oh, pretty good, man," he replied sheepishly. "Look, Ed, I know I still owe you some dough, and you'll get it all when I get completely back on my feet."

I pointed down and said, "Well, it's good to see you're preparing your feet for that moment by wearing those designer Italian shoes."

"Oh, uh, you know, I have to keep up my image since I'm in sales. Believe me, it's the only decent pair I own. They're Bruno Magli, you know, O.J.'s shoes."

"Oh, I wondered where the missing evidence went," I replied.

It was clear we were both uncomfortable, and Phillip mumbled, "Hey, I'd better get inside. Looking forward to your show!" and hurriedly disappeared into the building.

Steve said, "Wow, he took off in a hurry."

"Yeah, that's what $700 shoes will do for you," I offered.

Turk was aghast. "Those are $700? How do you know?"

"Because I paid for them."

It was rather odd that the event was held literally inside the museum. Not in a special room, or the auditorium, but the actual museum itself. This meant that people were wolfing down food and drink mere feet away from supposedly priceless works of art. There was an immense security force on hand to shoo people away whenever they got too close to the paintings. This gave the event an odd, Third Reich reception aura, as it was hard to relax when guys in headsets were eyeing everyone suspiciously during the entire evening. Of course, it was already hard for me to relax as it was, considering my bit of nervousness over speaking with Pam. Not to mention the usual stage nerves in anticipation of my little performance to come.

I asked Armando, the museum coordinator, where I

could find Pam, and he told me that she hadn't yet arrived. He did say he had her cell phone number and offered to call her to check her ETA. I said that wouldn't
be necessary; I'd just wait for her. Though internally I
was dying to talk to her, I had to keep my exterior cool. I
didn't want to appear too eager.

As was to be expected, there was plenty of awkward,
painful small talk, mostly people discussing the trials
and tribulations of their jobs. There were the mandatory
reunion occurrences: several guys coming out of the
closet, thinking they were surprising people even though
everyone knew they were gay twenty years ago; the guy
who kept introducing himself over and over to everybody, and saying "Hey, I remember you!" even to members of the Warhol Center staff who had never seen him
before in their lives; another guy taking a swing at someone who had hit him in the head with a Jolly Rancher
during freshman algebra.

My old high school friend alcohol was there, but
luckily I didn't feel the need to socialize with him. In
fact, it was blessedly easy to ignore him completely. But
he was plenty busy with many of my classmates, so I
don't think he missed me too much.

One of my favorite moments occurred when a classmate drunkenly told me that he never thought I would
really amount to anything and that he was pleasantly
surprised that I actually had done okay. He himself
owned his own business, apparently a little "backhanded

compliments" shop in town. I felt vindicated later when he accidentally brushed up against a painting and was beset by security who treated him like he'd just fired a shot at the Pope.

It was fascinating to see how people had aged over the years. There were those lucky few who somehow looked younger than they did back in school. On the other hand, there were also those who, while only in their late thirties, looked as though they had gone to school with Miss Jane Pittman.

One old classmate had worked for Bill Clinton in the White House and told me he might relocate to LA with the ex-president, who was considering working in show business. I remarked that I was somewhat surprised that Hollywood had so heartily embraced the post-Lewinsky Clinton. After all, these were the same people who made Pee Wee Herman a pariah because he masturbated in an adult theater. Sorry, Pee Wee, I guess lewd behavior is only acceptable if you have a high security clearance. Another classmate, Mark, had become "born again," and regaled me with the incredible details. He said that God had spoken to him through his car radio. I said, "Man, you must have a kick-ass radio. I can't even pick up the local campus station." Mark assured me it was true. He said it with such earnest conviction, the only thing I knew to do was . . . ridicule him. I asked, "What station, KGOD? Are you sure it wasn't just Casey Kasem? He's got a pretty deep voice." I could hear it now. "I'm

Casey Kasem with America's top ten commandments. Holding steady at number one, in its fifty thousandth week, 'Thou shall have no other gods before me!'"

Mark said that God had warned him that he was leading a sinful life. Now, unless Mark was involved in something I didn't know about, he seemed to be a pretty average guy. Back in high school, he partied a bit but was honest and nice, and had settled into a productive life as a real estate broker in Pittsburgh. He certainly seemed an odd choice for a warning by God over say, someone like Osama bin Laden. But maybe Osama only gets AM radio. Who knows? Maybe it really did happen. I didn't doubt God's ability to do such a thing. I just doubted the likelihood that he'd do it to Mark, in his Subaru, on the way back from a bowling alley.

There seemed to be a lot of the same conversations taking place that had occurred at the five-year reunion, except with a slightly different twist this time:

"What are you doing these days?"

"Oh, I have a couple kids, just got divorced. How about you?"

"Three kids, divorced a year."

The fact that nearly everybody had relationship problems of some sort was disconcerting, yet at the same time, oddly comforting. The thought struck me that perhaps I'd dodged a major bullet by not marrying Rita. So many classmates got married, then divorced, which was especially sad when children were involved. When I considered the emotional cost these folks had paid for their relationships, it made my cost of failure with Rita seem not that high, at least in comparison. In fact, it looked suspiciously like the proverbial blessing in disguise. Wow, where had that mature thought come from? Was that gravy at last trickling onto the last dry, holdout area in my life?

A voice behind me shouted, "There's Ed Driscoll, Hollywood hunk!" I turned to see that it was Pam. She walked over and greeted me with a warm embrace.

I said, "Hey, I've been waiting for you!"

She said, "And I've been waiting for you, for longer than you know!"

Well, if I'd subconsciously had any doubt about her feelings for me, they certainly were gone now.

"I'm so glad you're here," she gushed. "I've got everything set up for you. Let me show you." She took me by the arm and walked me into the auditorium, where everything was perfectly in place. I thanked her for organizing everything so well. I told her that she'd be surprised at how many people just assume that a comedian can perform anywhere and that amenities such as lighting, sound, and sight lines don't mean anything.

Pam said, "You're going to do great, like you always do. Thank you so much for doing this!" and gave me another big hug. She then excused herself to the main hallway where everyone was mingling and spoke into the public address system, announcing that my show would begin in fifteen minutes.

My classmates made their way to the auditorium. As they filed in, I suddenly began getting nervous. Geez, what if I bombed? After all, it happens to the best of us. What if people suddenly resent me for interrupting their pleasant social gathering? Everyone seemed to be enjoying themselves, catching up with each other; did they really want to listen to me? And worst of all, what if I tanked in front of Pam? It was the usual case of pre-performance nerves, now amplified by the pressure of being in front of my peers, including one I was interested in romantically.

I tried to push the negative thoughts out of my mind as I was introduced, but as luck would have it, the microphone in the auditorium suddenly stopped working. I fought desperately to not take this as a sign of an inevitable debacle about to occur. The fact that there was no sound amplification actually had the unintended effect of forcing everyone to be especially quiet if they wanted to hear me. This helped keep a semblance of order I had been afraid might not be possible given the length of the cocktail "hour" we'd just had.

Fortunately, people were very receptive, even when I opened in typically sardonic fashion with the observation that we were all lucky to have gone to high school in an era when slaying your classmates wasn't yet hip. I remarked that it would be pretty easy to put together the short list of people most likely to have done so and that some of them were here tonight. People responded with dark laughter when I said the most we all had to worry about back then was being hit with a dodgeball during gym class.

This segued nicely into my good-natured mockery of a classmate who was now a postal worker. I asked him why shooting co-workers was such a popular method of expressing job dissatisfaction in his occupation. After all, I asked, whatever happened to good, old-fashioned, backstabbing gossip to bring down a fellow employee? It's been a tried-and-true method for years, so why the need for Gatling guns all of a sudden? But I told him that as a result, I, for one, certainly don't complain any-more when my *Newsweek* is delivered in fifteen sepa-rate pieces or my swimsuit issue of *Sports Illustrated* arrives with what I hope to God are only thumbprints all over it.

As laughter filled the auditorium, my eyes were drawn to Pam, who was standing in the back of the room, chuckling and nodding her approval. I felt great, totally in control, completely in my element. As I performed, my mind drifted and embarked on its own independent journey, an out-of-body type of experience. It was as though I were standing in the front row, watching my-self and thinking that this was truly a gravy moment. I was filled with the cognizance of just how lucky I was to be able to do what I love for a living and to be able to share it with friends and classmates. Despite the deep-rooted cynicism that for some reason had been a major part of my makeup from early youth, a cynicism I often employed in my art, I suddenly understood how much serendipity surrounded my life. I realized and was thankful for all the momentous opportunities that following my dream had made possible for me.

The feeling of contentment that settled over me was unlike anything I'd ever experienced before, the sort of serenity that can't be delivered by any outside agent, such as booze or sex or money. This kind of tranquility could only come from within.

My mind slowly rejoined my body up onstage, and after twenty-five minutes or so, I said good night and bounded off the stage to thunderous applause.

Pam was the first to greet me with a big hug, saying, "Ed, that was great, but I expected nothing less!" Then, indicating a grinning man standing beside her, she continued, "I want to introduce you to my fiancé, Morris."

I was floored. At first, I didn't know how to react. But here's what happened next. I punched Morris in the mouth, told Pam she represented all that is wrong with the female species, then went on a drinking binge that climaxed with me back onstage in the auditorium, screaming incoherently at my stunned ex-classmates while simultaneously giving them the finger. Several tense, violent minutes later, security managed to drag me, kicking and screaming, off to the city jail.

Yep, that's what happened next, in my mind. But in the real world, I merely stuck out my hand to this man now standing with his arm around Pam and pretended not to be stunned.

"Wow, fiancé, huh?" I managed to squeak out. "Last I talked to you, you weren't even dating anyone."

"I know, it happened really fast. We met just two weeks ago and, well, we just knew right away."

I congratulated them as insouciantly as I could. Her fiancé said, "Hey, you were really good, dude." Wow, that sure meant a lot to me at that point. Pam thanked me again for doing the show, and I told her that I was glad I hadn't disappointed her. Wouldn't she have been surprised if she knew that she had actually disappointed me?

Well, wasn't this super? How could I go from feeling so good to feeling so terrible, so damn fast? And here I thought I'd been stupid for not picking up obvious signs of her interest sooner. It turns out I'd been even more stupid for actually picking up "obvious" signs of her interest. Thank God, at least I hadn't talked to Pam about what I'd erroneously thought were her romantic overtures. I shuddered at the thought of how humiliating that conversation would have been.

I was surprised, disgusted, disappointed, and tired. Why the hell had I even left Los Angeles? I should have known better. I considered asking Steve to drop me home right then, but I didn't want to wreck his good time. I briefly entertained the thought of grabbing a cab, but that would've looked weird to people. After all, nobody knew that I was upset, and I saw no need for anyone to find out. I'd just have to tough it out for the remainder of the event.

I sat off in a corner of the museum for a while, contemplating this hellish turn of events. Occasionally, a classmate would wander over, and I'd put on as much of a happy face as I could muster until he or she moved on to mingle.

I eventually meandered outside onto the sidewalk to get some air, and a friendly, very pretty woman came outside and struck up a conversation with me. Though I hadn't really felt like talking, she was unusually easy to converse with, very witty, and very smart. The bad part was she wasn't wearing a name tag, and I couldn't remember who the hell she was. I felt stupid but finally summoned up enough courage to say, "Please forgive me, but I just don't remember your name."

She looked hurt, then said, "You're kidding me. After all those classes we had together, you don't know who I am? I'm Laura!" Panicked, I said, "Oh, yes, of course, Laura. But, uh, I can't quite place your last name; it's been a few years and all."

She burst out laughing. "I can't do this to you," she giggled. "I didn't go to your school."

Now I really felt stupid, especially since I'd pretended that I did remember her. "Wow, what did I do to deserve that?" I asked.

"Nothing at all, I'm sorry," she continued.

Despite being made a fool of, I couldn't help but be a bit smitten.

"Well, if you didn't go to our school, I'm afraid I'll have to ask you to leave. Don't make me summon security," I told her.

She laughed and said, "I'm here with my cousin. I was in town, and he couldn't find a real date."

"You look like a real date to me," I offered. "So who's your cousin?"

"Phillip Johnson. You know him, don't you?"

Know him? Know him? Yeah, I know that . . .

"Ah, yes, of course I do. I saw him briefly in the parking lot. He's actually a good friend. How's he doing?"

"Oh, fine." She sighed, then continued. "Well, between you and me, not as good as he'd like everyone to think. His business hasn't been doing well. In fact, he borrowed a bunch of money from my dad just to keep himself afloat this year."

"Really?"

"Yeah, but please don't tell him I told you. He's very proud."

"He's not that proud," I muttered.

"What?"

"Uh, nothing. So, your dad was cool with that?"

"Oh, yeah, he knows Phil's a good guy. And Phil did pay him back every cent. And obviously his business is doing a little better, because he hasn't borrowed any more money from Dad."

"Well, uh, yeah, good for him."

"The bad part is, he spent money he shouldn't have to rent a nice car and buy these fancy clothes, just because he was so hung up on how he'd look in front of his old classmates. Kind of shallow, huh?"

No. Not at all. Just kind of human.

As the reunion wound down, Laura and I decided to continue our conversation over some late-night coffee. I found out some important things about her, such as her occupation (events planner), where she lived (New York City), and oh yeah, her last name (Collins). We made plans for lunch the next afternoon, which then turned into dinner. By the time we flew back to our respective cities, we'd put together plans for her to come out and visit me in LA. What a strange reversal of circumstances. I had arrived at the reunion wondering if Phillip would pay me back, but left the reunion feeling like I actually owed him.

Chapter
⁋ 10 ⁋

Post-reunion:
Forward to the Past

I stepped through the doors of Quality Carats in Beverly Hills with my new fiancée. I realized it was probably inviting bad vibes, the very thing I usually went out of my way to avoid. But I figured I could at least use the $4,000 credit they had given me toward a new ring. Ron was bemused to see me and smugly asked if this was the "lucky lady." I said, "Lucky? I'm not sure I'd call her that, but this is my fiancée, Laura."

I told Laura that she could pick out any ring she desired, and she began wandering the store, wide-eyed. Once she was out of earshot, I pulled Ron aside.

"Look, the only reason I even came back here was to use my store credit of four grand. I still resent what you did to me." Ron said, "Hey, there's no reason for any hostility. I only did what I could do; I don't set the rules for the jewelry business. I just abide by them, because I have to. I'll tell you what, I'll increase your credit to $5,000 toward a new ring. You have a lovely new bride-to-be, a new life starting, so there's no reason you and I can't have a new beginning as well. What do you say?"

Aw, hell, I thought, *he's right.* I realized that he's just another person trying to earn a living, and after all, he wasn't the one who invented the greedy, consumer-gouging diamond industry. I guess I should no more blame him personally than I should blame the guy who runs the corner Mobil station for high gasoline prices. And, he was right; it was time for me to make my new beginning a positive one. We shook hands.

As we did so, Laura let out a squeal of delight from across the store. Apparently, she'd found the perfect ring. She pulled me over to the display case and pointed out the source of her excitement. It was a beautiful piece, sparkling like . . . well, like a big freakin' diamond. It rested in a really elegant setting. Though as I've said before, I'm not really much into jewelry, I had to admit it was perfect. If I absolutely *had* to buy a ring, this is the one I'd buy. But the problem was, I already had. It was Rita's ring, the one I had sold back to Ron.

"Oh, honey, I love it, but I didn't see how expensive it is," Laura cooed. "I can't ask you to do that." I looked at the price tag next to it, which read "$23,000." Steadying myself, I told Laura that nothing in the world was too good for her. (The most frightening part about it was, I meant it.) I told Laura that I'd like to talk to Ron for a moment, and pulled him aside.

"That's my ring, man!" I actually yelled in a whisper, if

one can do that. Ron said, "No, it isn't. But it can be for $23,000."

"That's more than I paid the first time!" I hissed. "Plus, I sold it to you for $6,000 plus a $5,000 credit toward more jewelry."

"That's $4,000 toward other jewelry," Ron corrected me.

"You just said five!"

"I can't give you $5,000 off of a gem like that," Ron replied. "But, with your four grand discount, you can get it for $19,000."

I was outraged. "No fucking way!" I sputtered. "I'm going to tell her what you're doing to me."

"Go ahead," Ron said coolly. "I'm sure she'd love to hear that you were willing to spend $20,000 on that exact ring for your first fiancée, but not $19,000 on it for her." This stopped me dead in my tracks. Well, so much for my "new beginning" with Ron.

I ponied up the $19,000. The look on Laura's face was worth twice that. Which was a good thing, because twice that is pretty much what I ended up paying for it. Oh, well, when you've found your soul mate, no price is too high. Laura is everything I could want in a woman. She's a lover, a companion, a friend—even a football-watching buddy! She possesses a naturally optimistic outlook, and in marked contrast to Rita, and most other women I've been involved with, she's a calming influence on me.

As an example, a few weeks earlier we had flown to Florida, where I met her parents for the first time. There was a ridiculous snafu at the airport, and we had to wait hours to board our flight. As I began to get irritated, she turned to me, smiled, and said, "Hey, this delay is actually a good thing." "How's that?" I asked. "Well, it's just more time we can spend together." How could I argue with that?

I really knew we had a better than average chance of staying together when, after watching me do a routine on television about my breakup with Rita, Laura turned to me and laughingly said, "Wow, I'll never break up with you. I'm afraid you'll talk about me!"

It's incredible that I managed to find her. But, hey, didn't I always say I knew I'd find my true love, and it would conquer all?

≋ ≋

Wow, in love and engaged. I've been here before. But it's different this time. Laura isn't Rita, and I'm no longer Ed, at least not the Ed I was a year ago. For the most part, I've lost my fear of the future, which allows me to go forward and be a better person. There's no question that programmed into all of us is a basic biological need for sex, companionship, love. After my breakup with Rita, I viewed that "programming" as a curse, an unfortunate mistake in human physiology. I just couldn't, or wouldn't, see the opportunities for human development that the programming actually offered.

After Rita and I split, I lost all faith in ever finding a meaningful relationship. Despite having learned to be grateful for the gravy in other areas of my life, I just couldn't apply that precept to male/female relationships. In fact, instead of being grateful for the happy times Rita and I spent together, I was filled with nothing but regret for having met her in the first place. I considered every moment spent with her a waste of time. Even the happiest moments we shared seemed nowhere near worth the horrible pain that ensued when we broke up.

Yet even in spite of such feelings, I found myself "back up on the horse" quite often, as I went on torturous blind dates arranged by friends, grappled with Internet dating, and went out with some nice women I just didn't quite synchronize with. I then thought I had perhaps found my match as I pursued Pam. But despite being unceremoniously tossed off the steed again by Pam's fiancé revelation, I climbed almost immediately back up in the saddle vis-à-vis Laura. Despite apparently being the world's worst jockey, I seemed determined to win at least one relationship race.

It became clear that if I merely wanted to date casually for the rest of my life, I could avoid a lot of hassles. But because I was looking to settle down with just one person, disappointments were inevitable, until I found that one, who turned out to be Laura. Of course, she's not perfect, and of course, neither am I, which ironically makes us . . . perfect for each other. Without question, we'll experience the ups and downs that all relationships provide, but I'm better suited to handle it now. Plus, Laura's taught me about talking to each other, trusting each other, and not being afraid of risking one's feelings. These elements are critical, even if they eventually lead to acute pain, whether it's breaking up and having to go separate ways, or staying together and being forced to attend someone's baby shower. At last I've learned that more pain, while obviously more painful, also means more growth.

I hope Laura and I will live happily ever after. But all I can do is concentrate on today, on where I am right now. And I finally realize, it's not a bad place to be. In fact, it's pretty damn good.

Pass the gravy.

Chapter

≋ 11 ≋

It's Never Square
to Come Full Circle

I dialed a number that I hadn't called in over a year. Though I was conscious of what I was doing, I was still jolted when Rita answered the phone.

"Hello?"

"Uh, hey, Rita, guess who?"

There was a moment of silence, and I suddenly wondered if I'd made a mistake.

"Well, hi, Ed. I'm sorry, I'm just a bit taken back. You were pretty much the last person I expected to be calling."

"Yeah, but you know what the scary part is?" I made my voice sound like that of Vincent Price. *"I'm calling from inside the house!"* Rita cracked up, which momentarily took my breath away. I'd forgotten how nice her laugh was. Collecting myself, I forged ahead.

"Seriously, I don't mean to bother you. I guess I just wanted to say, I'm sorry about the way things ended."

"Well, me too, of course," she replied, sounding somewhat surprised.

"Well, uh, anyway," I stammered. "I just wanted to say, I realize that what happened to us was really nobody's fault. Things just didn't work out, and it happens. Relationships are difficult, but we did the best we could, don't you think?"

"Yes," she answered softly.

"Anyway," I continued, "I wish you nothing but the best, and I hope you're happy."

Rita was silent for a moment, then said, "Wow, it sounds like somebody's really grown up."

I laughed and said, "Yeah, well, it just took me a little longer than most. But forty is a pretty cute age anyway, don't you think?"

We talked a little longer, then said our good-byes, and as I hung up the phone, I felt as if someone had just removed the universe from the top of my shoulders.

About the Author

Ed Driscoll is an Emmy Award–winning comedian, writer, and producer. A bright and clever stand-up comic known for his quick wit, Ed has appeared on television programs such as *Politically Incorrect* and *NBC's Comedy Showcase*. Driscoll is a highly sought "punch-up" writer, contributing to various television shows such as *The Drew Carey Show*, television specials such as *The Academy Awards*, and various feature films such as *Scooby-Doo, The Lizzie McGuire Movie,* and *National Security*. His recent movie *The Comeback*, starring Samuel L. Jackson, won Best Short Film at the 2002 Aspen Comedy Festival. Driscoll is based in Los Angeles.

Please visit his Web site, www.driscomic.com, for more information.

Hazelden Publishing and Educational Services is a division of the Hazelden Foundation, a not-for-profit organization. Since 1949, Hazelden has been a leader in promoting the dignity and treatment of people afflicted with the disease of chemical dependency.

The mission of the foundation is to improve the quality of life for individuals, families, and communities by providing a national continuum of information, education, and recovery services that are widely accessible; to advance the field through research and training; and to improve our quality and effectiveness through continuous improvement and innovation.

Stemming from that, the mission of this division is to provide quality information and support to people wherever they may be in their personal journey—from education and early intervention, through treatment and recovery, to personal and spiritual growth.

Although our treatment programs do not necessarily use everything Hazelden publishes, our bibliotherapeutic materials support our mission and the Twelve Step philosophy upon which it is based. We encourage your comments and feedback.

The headquarters of the Hazelden Foundation are in Center City, Minnesota. Additional treatment facilities are located in Chicago, Illinois; Newberg, Oregon; New York, New York; Plymouth, Minnesota; and St. Paul, Minnesota. At these sites, we provide a continuum of care for men and women of all ages. Our Plymouth facility is designed specifically for youth and families.

For more information on Hazelden, please call **1-800-257-7800.** Or you may access our World Wide Web site on the Internet at **www.hazelden.org.**